Mystical Cats

This book belongs to

____

COLORING AND MEDITATION CATS

Lisa Faganello

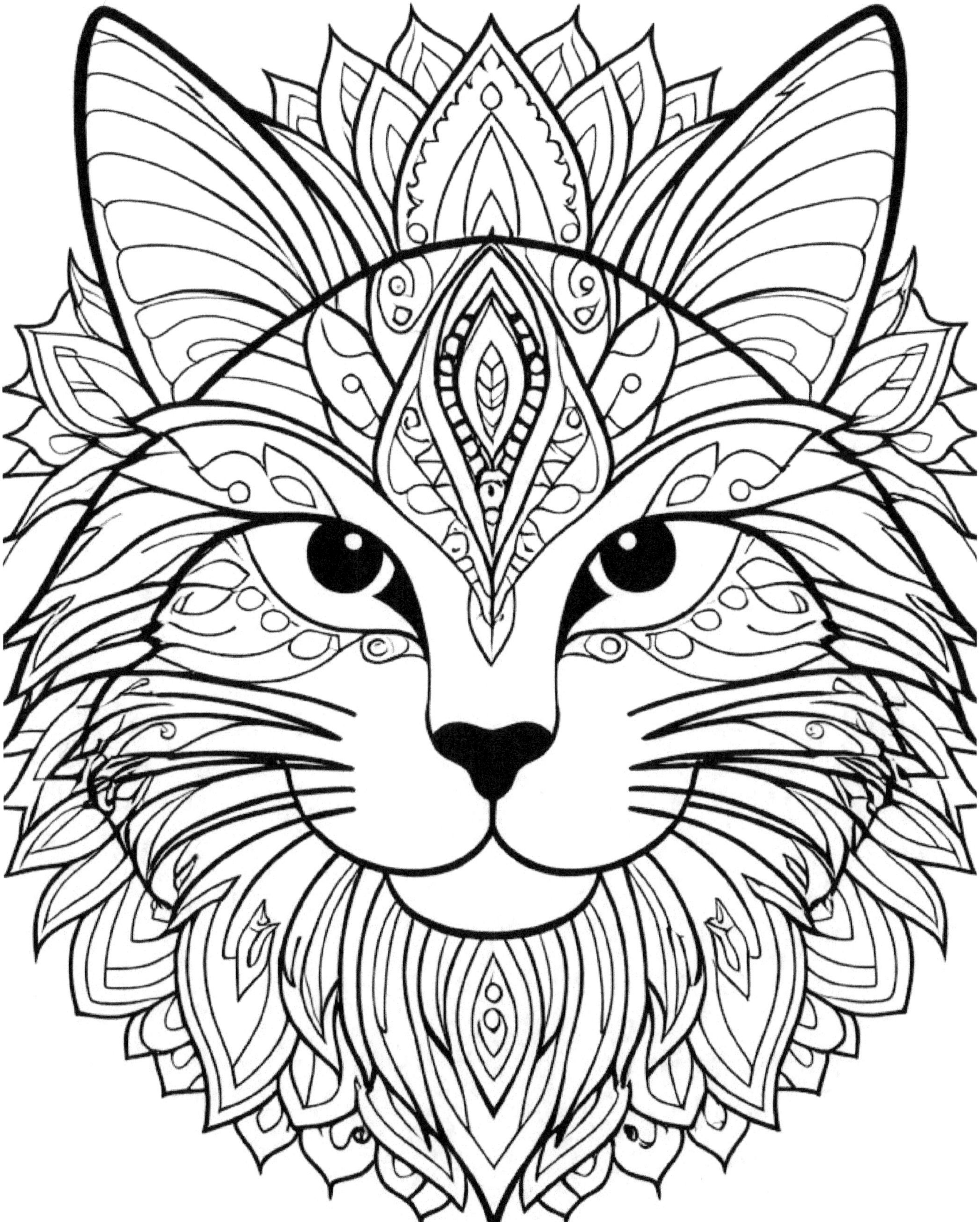

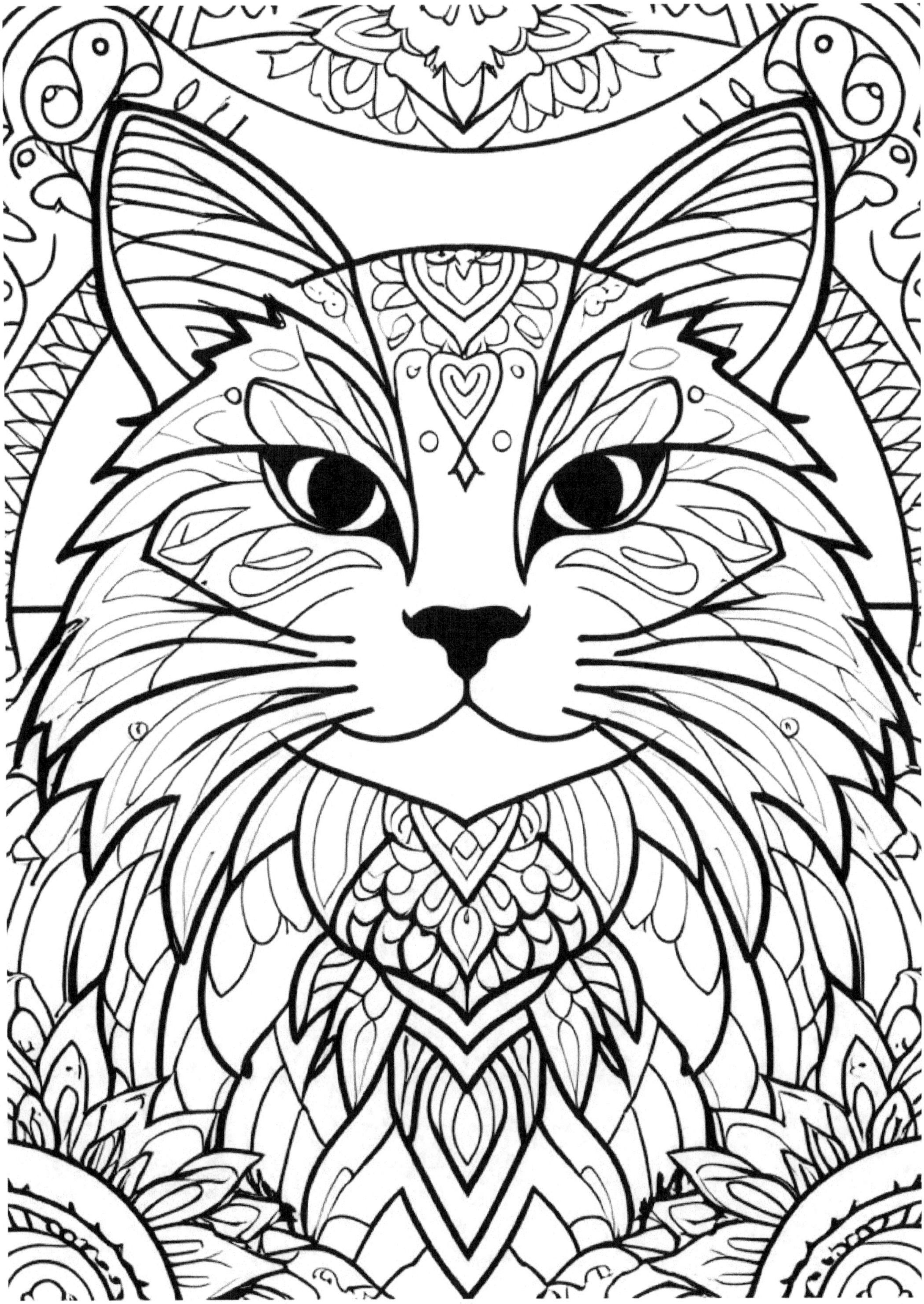

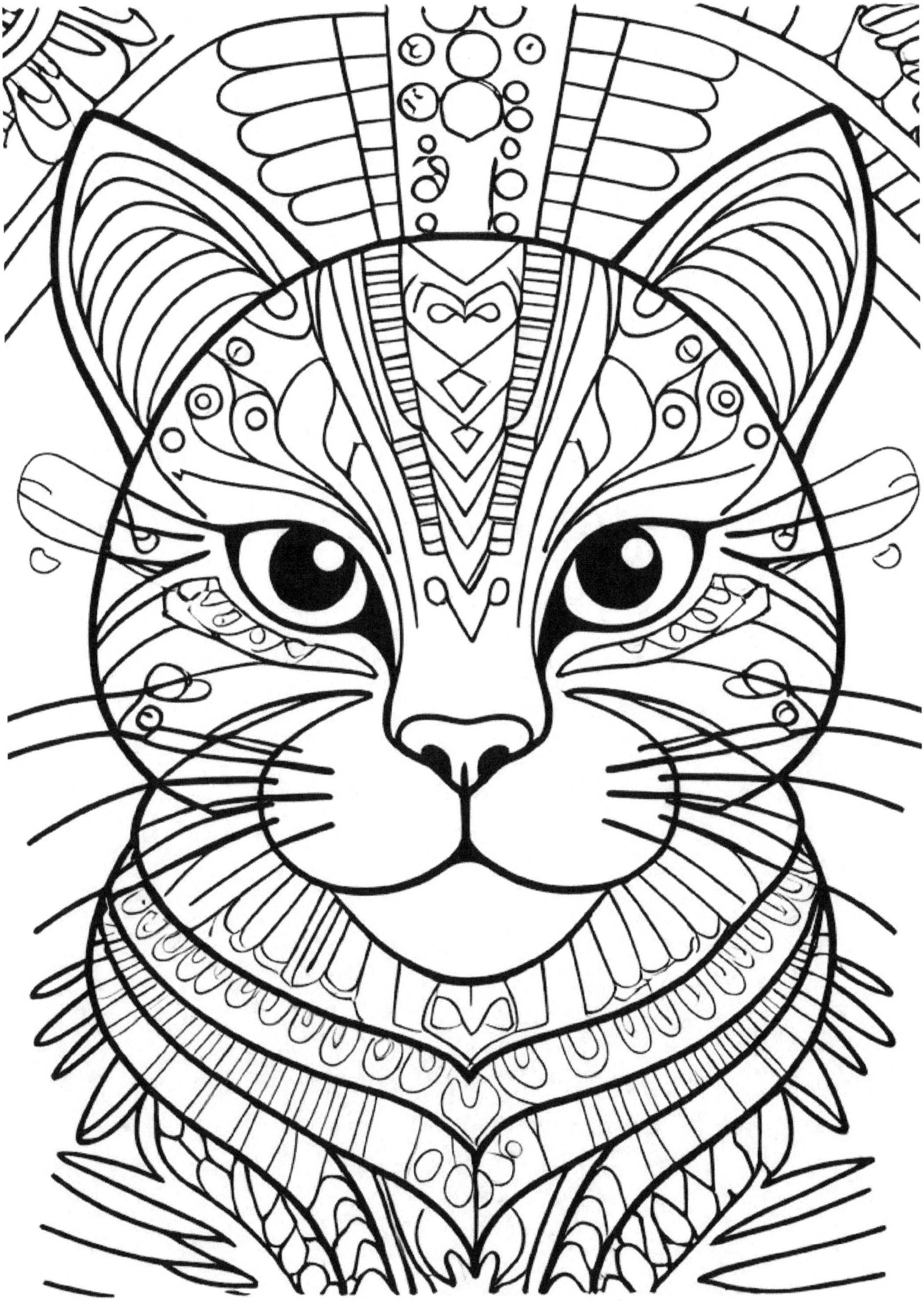

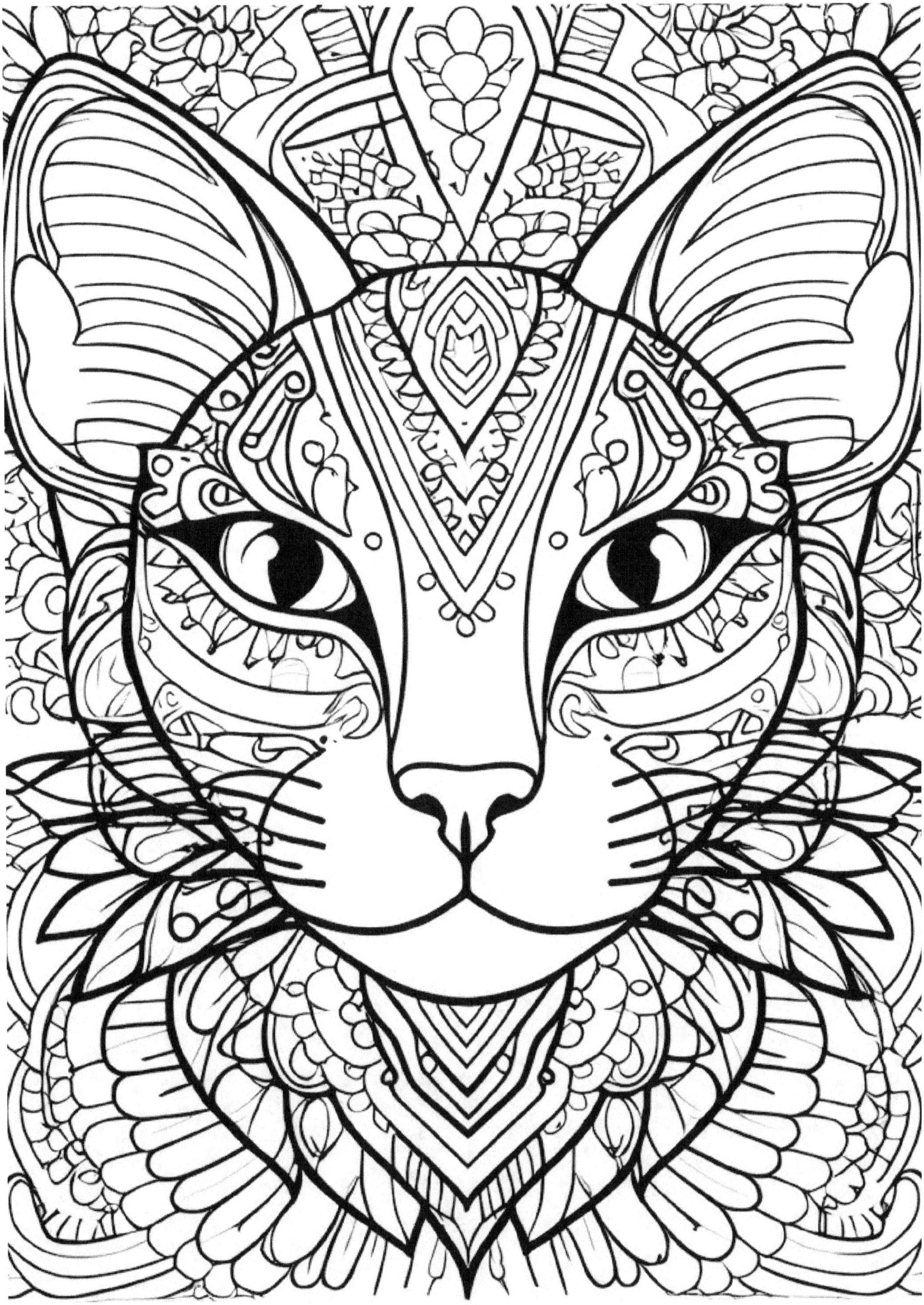

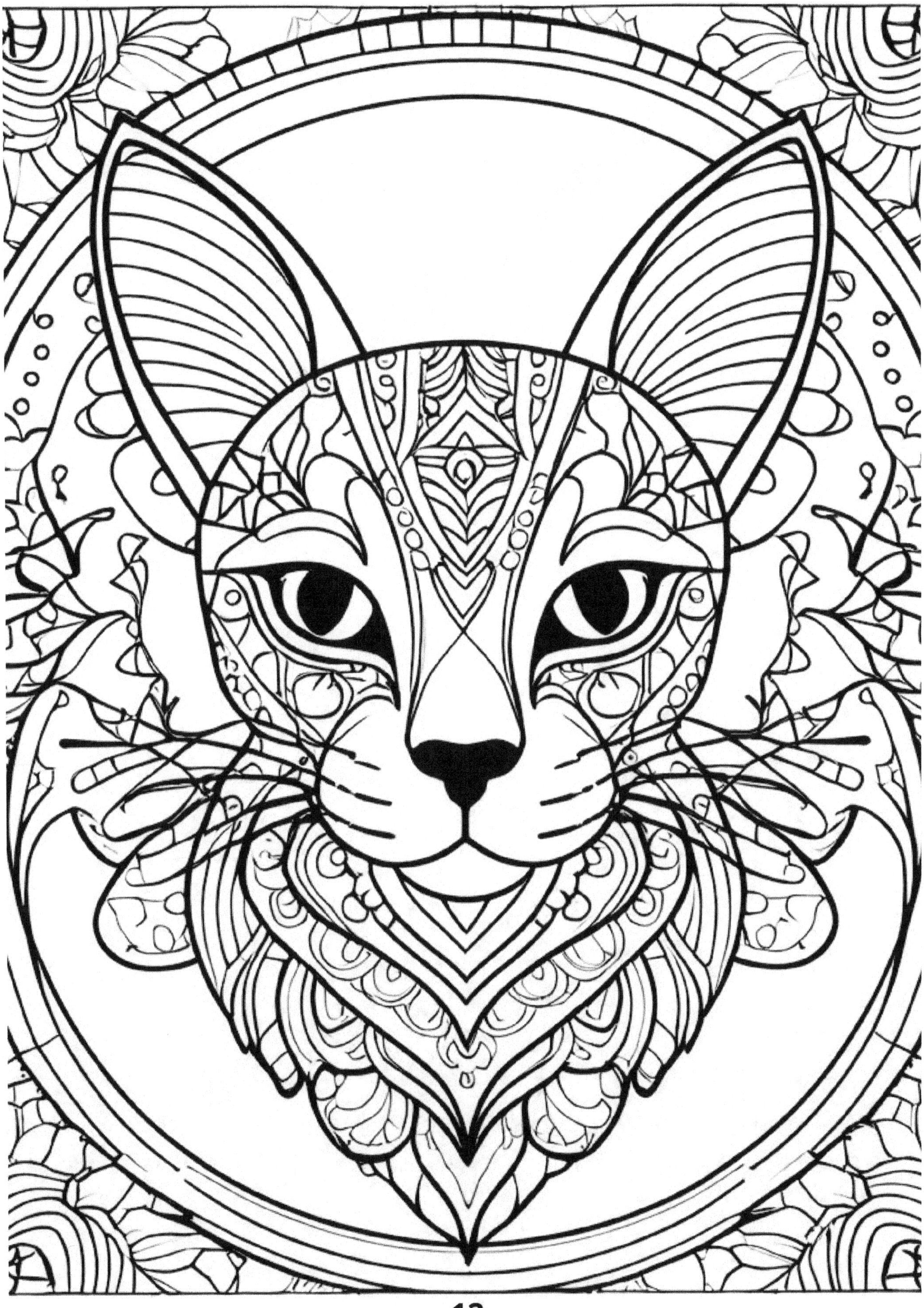

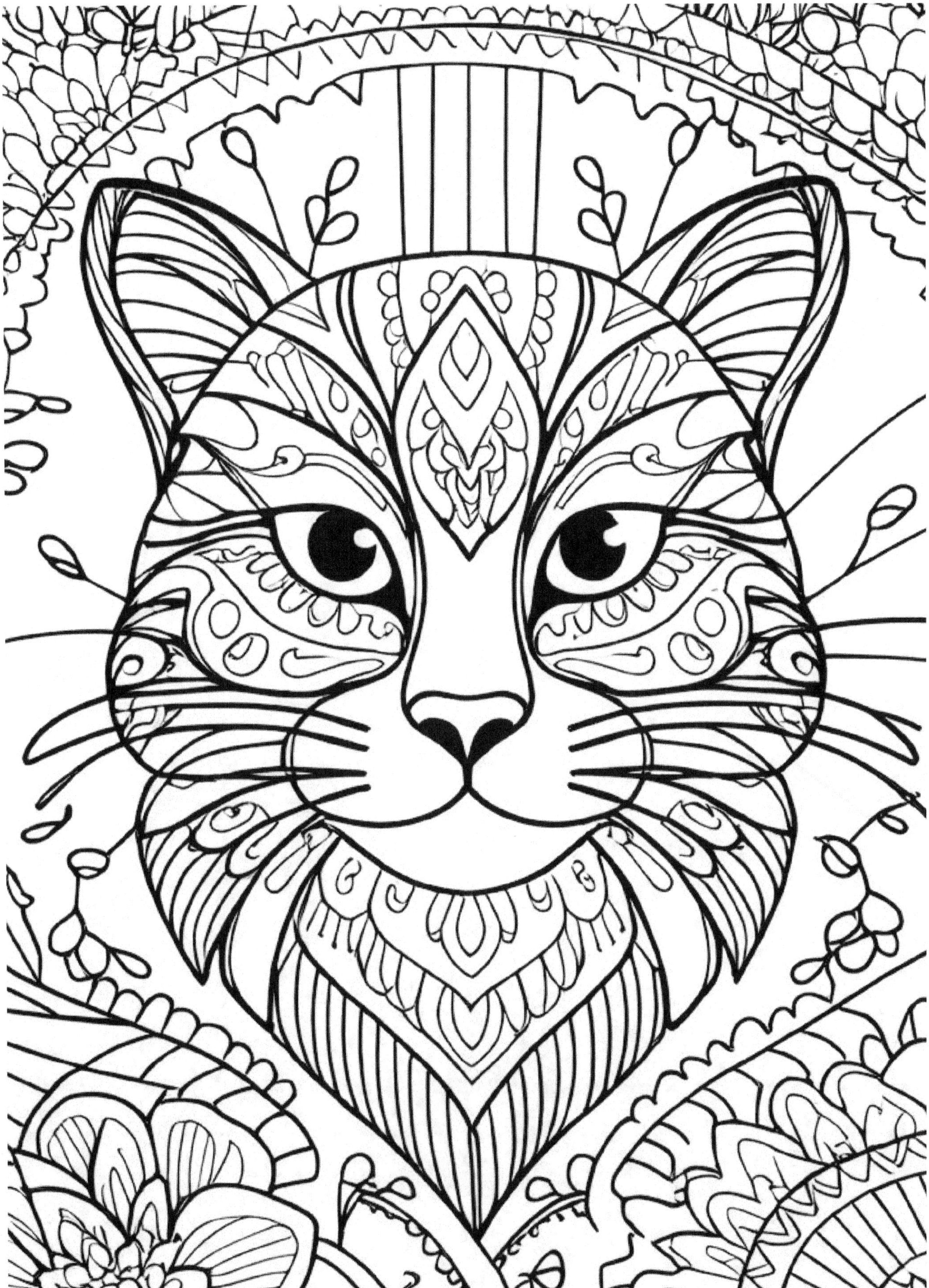

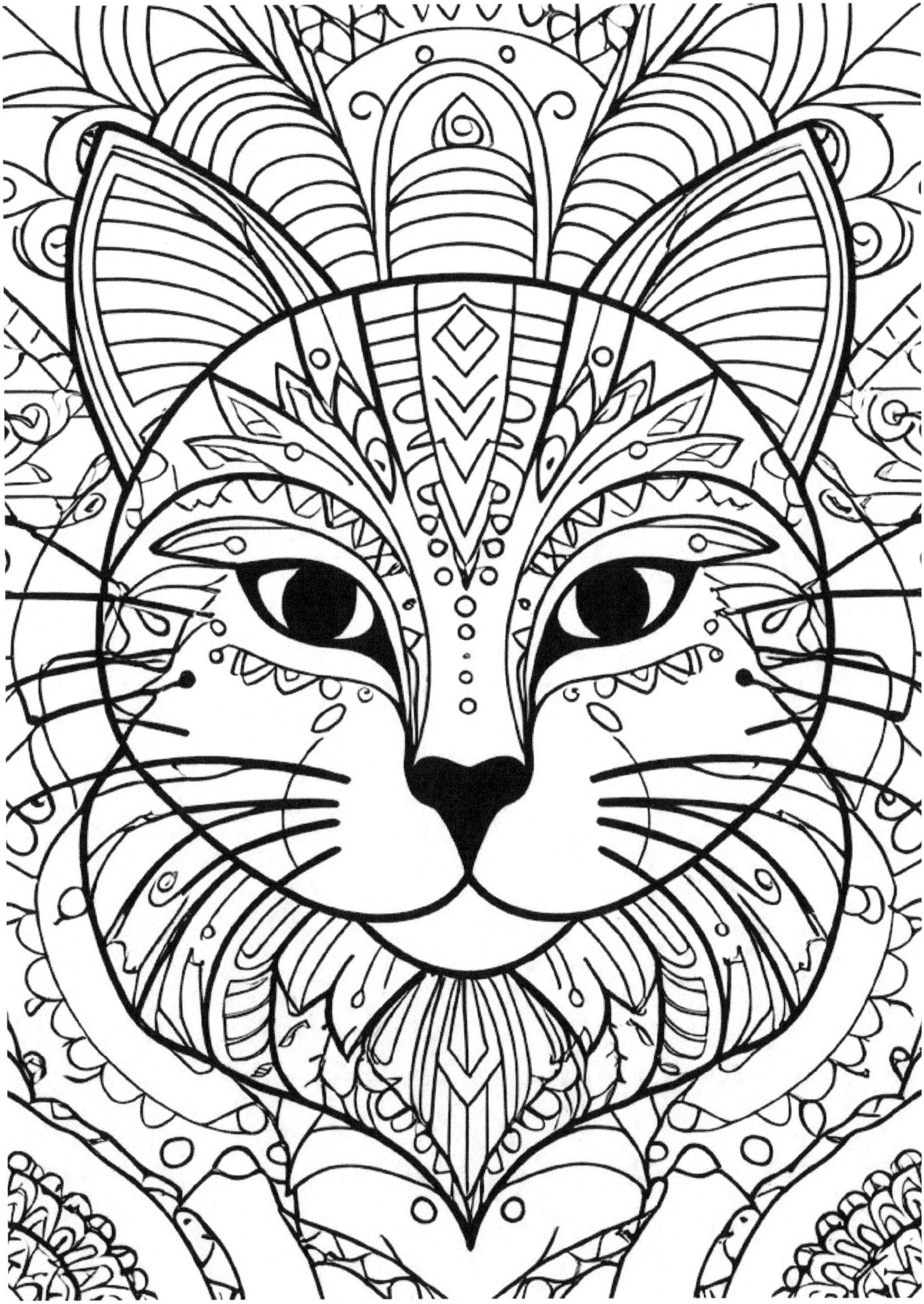

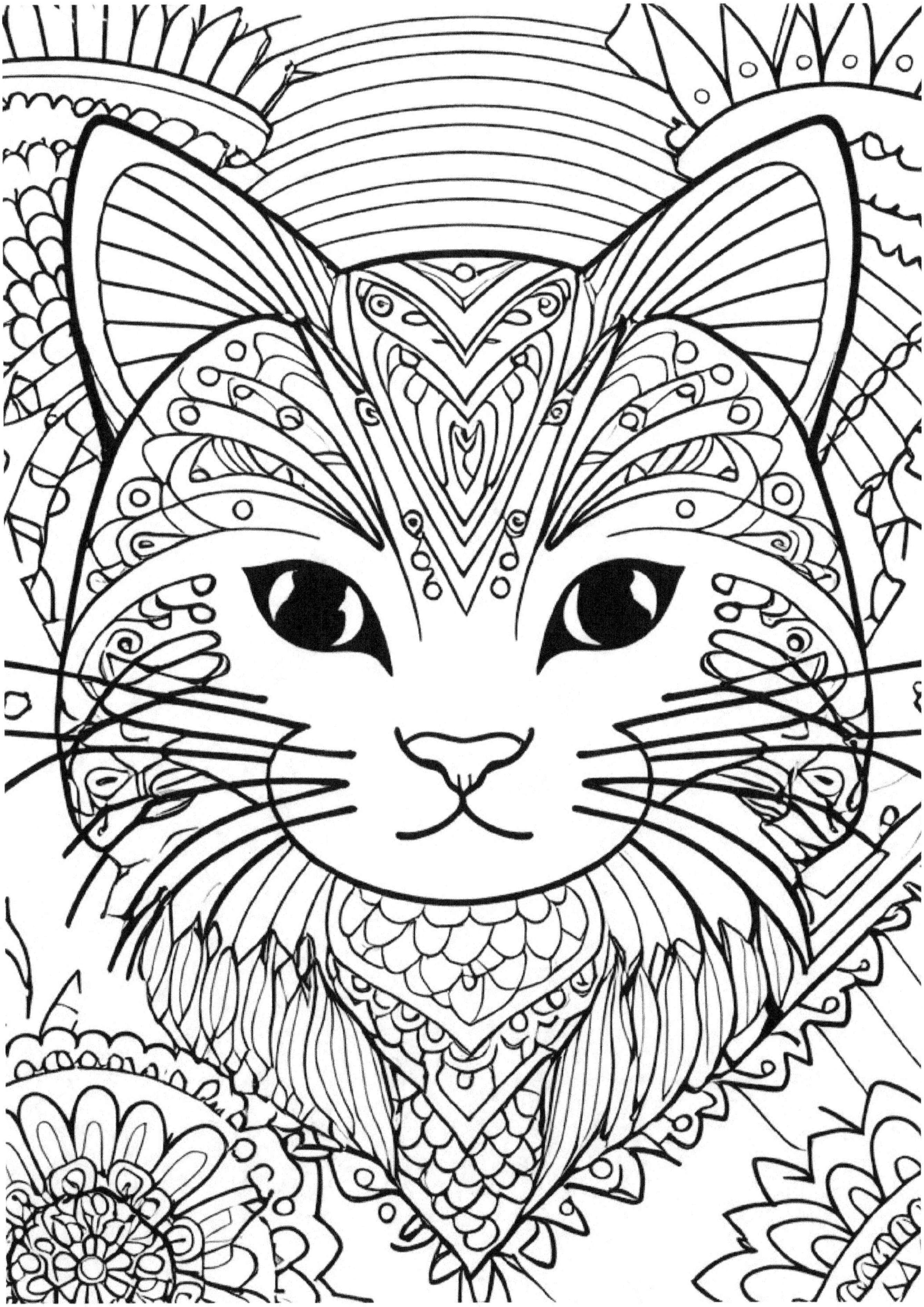

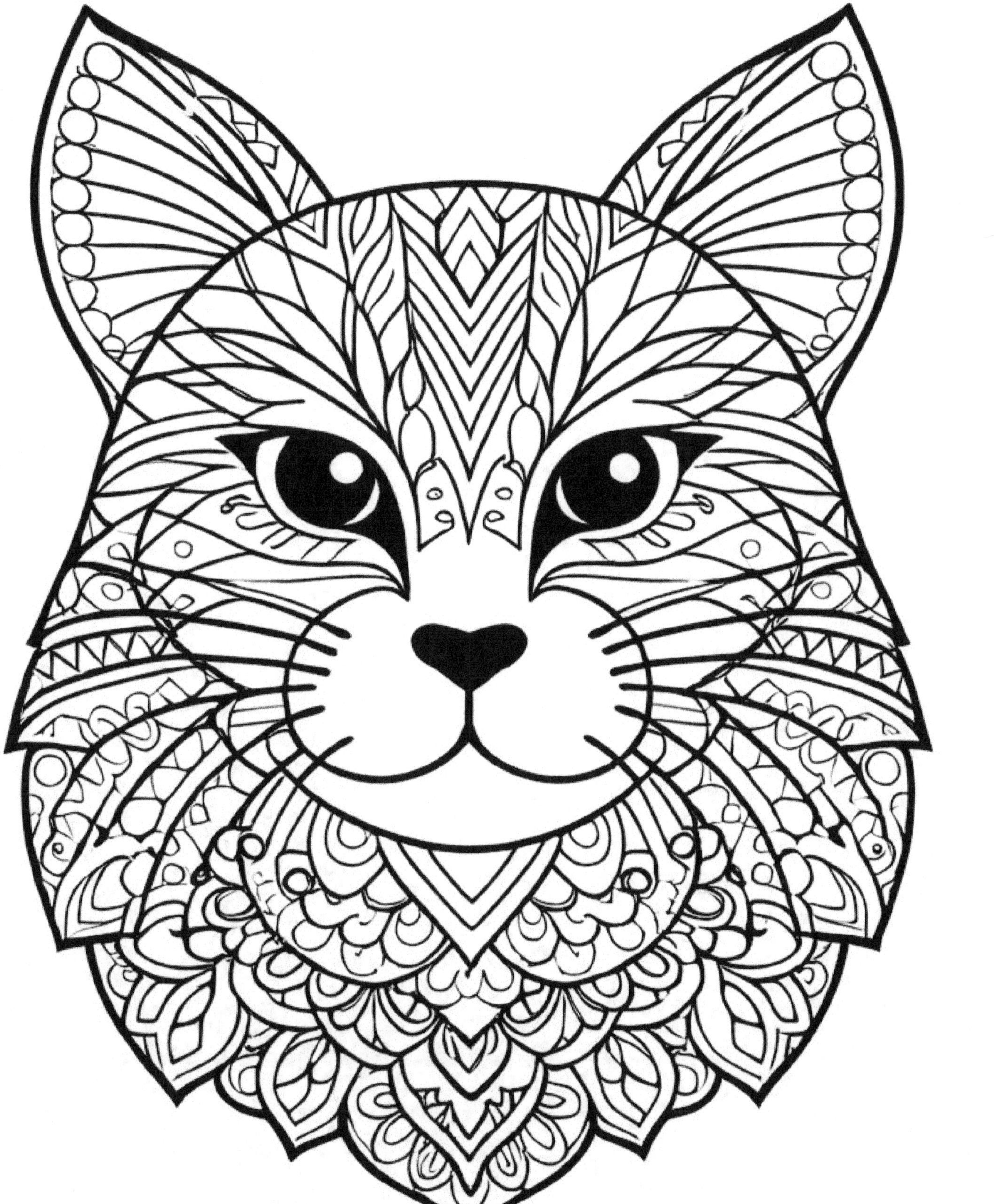

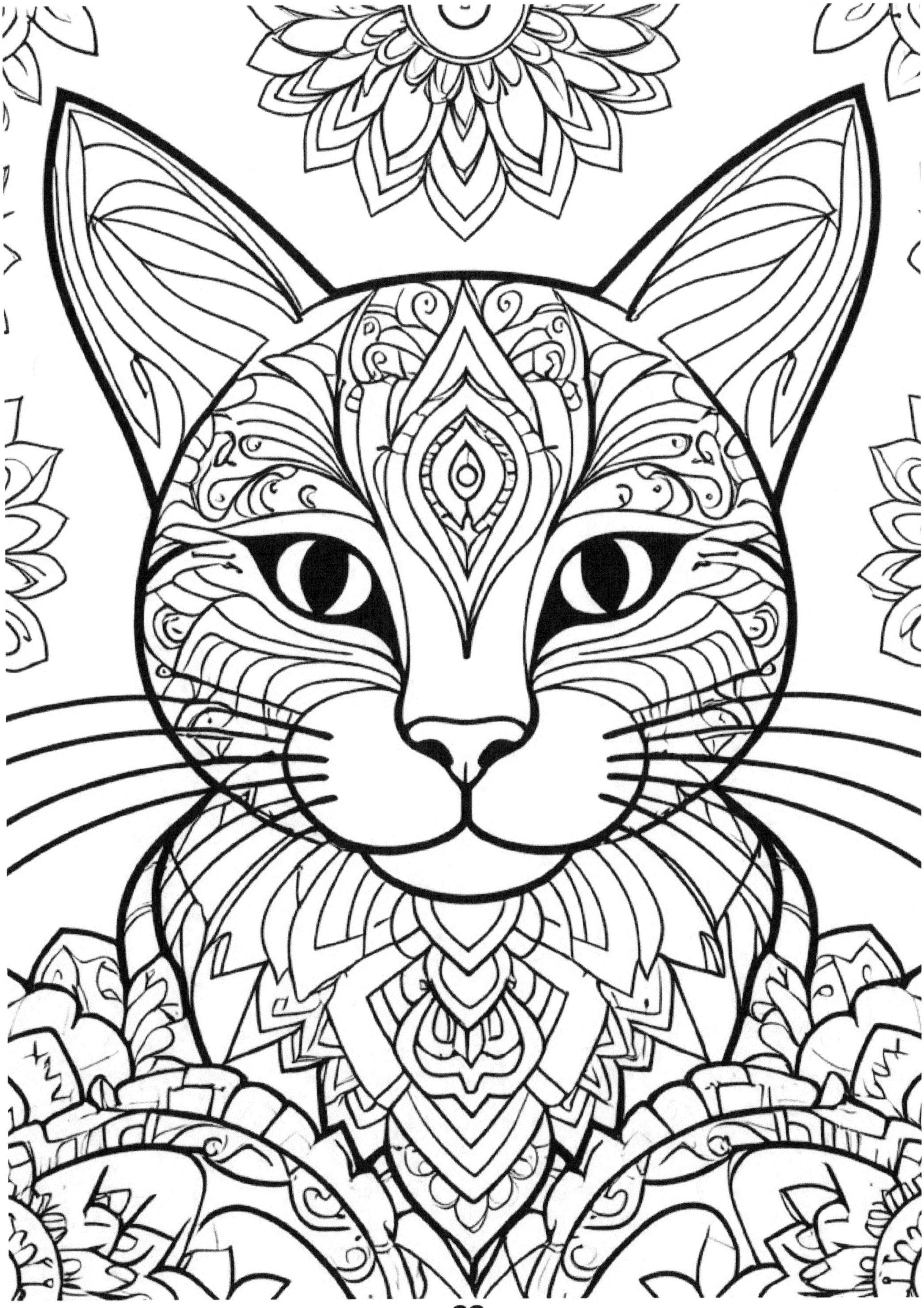

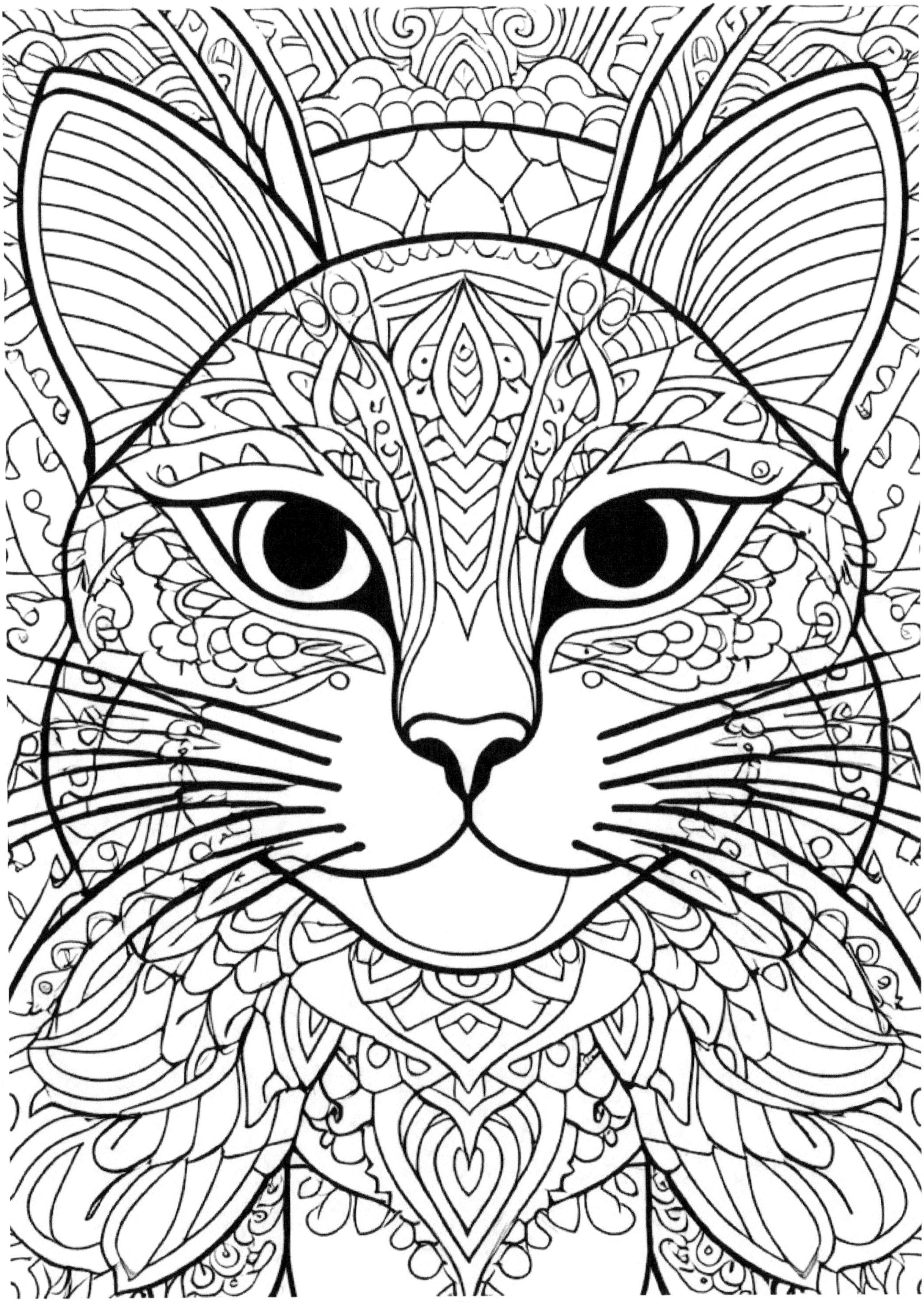

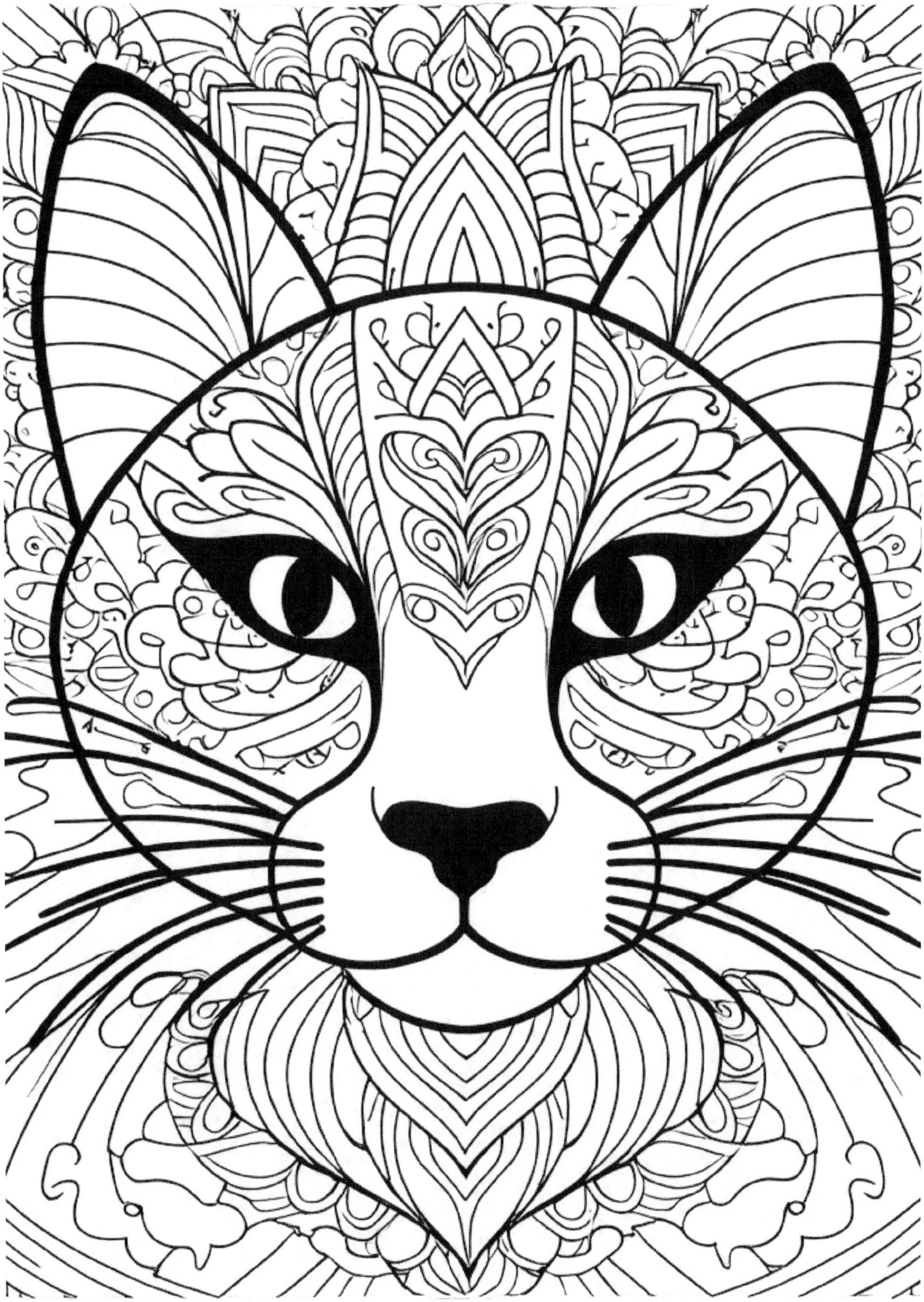

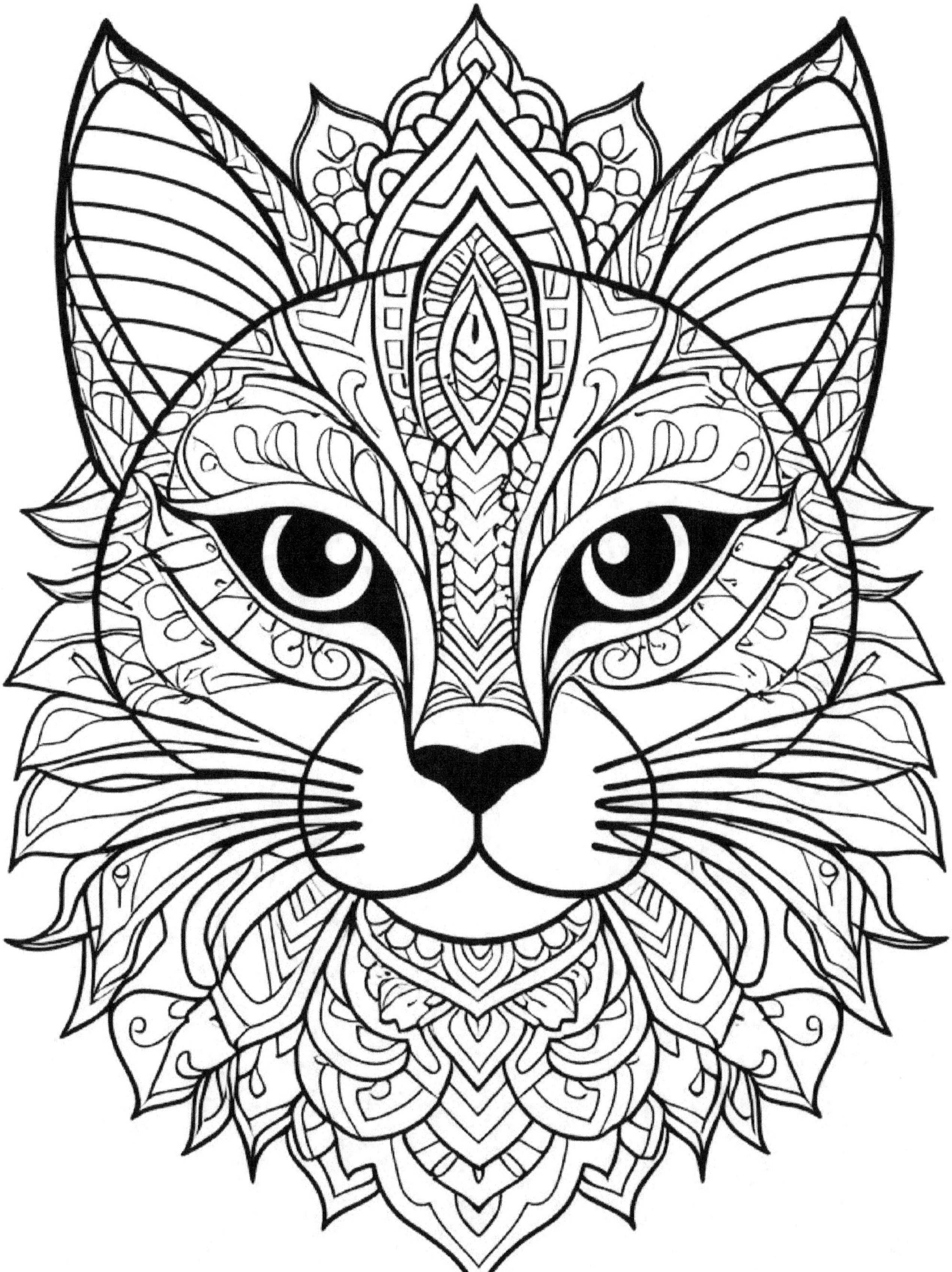

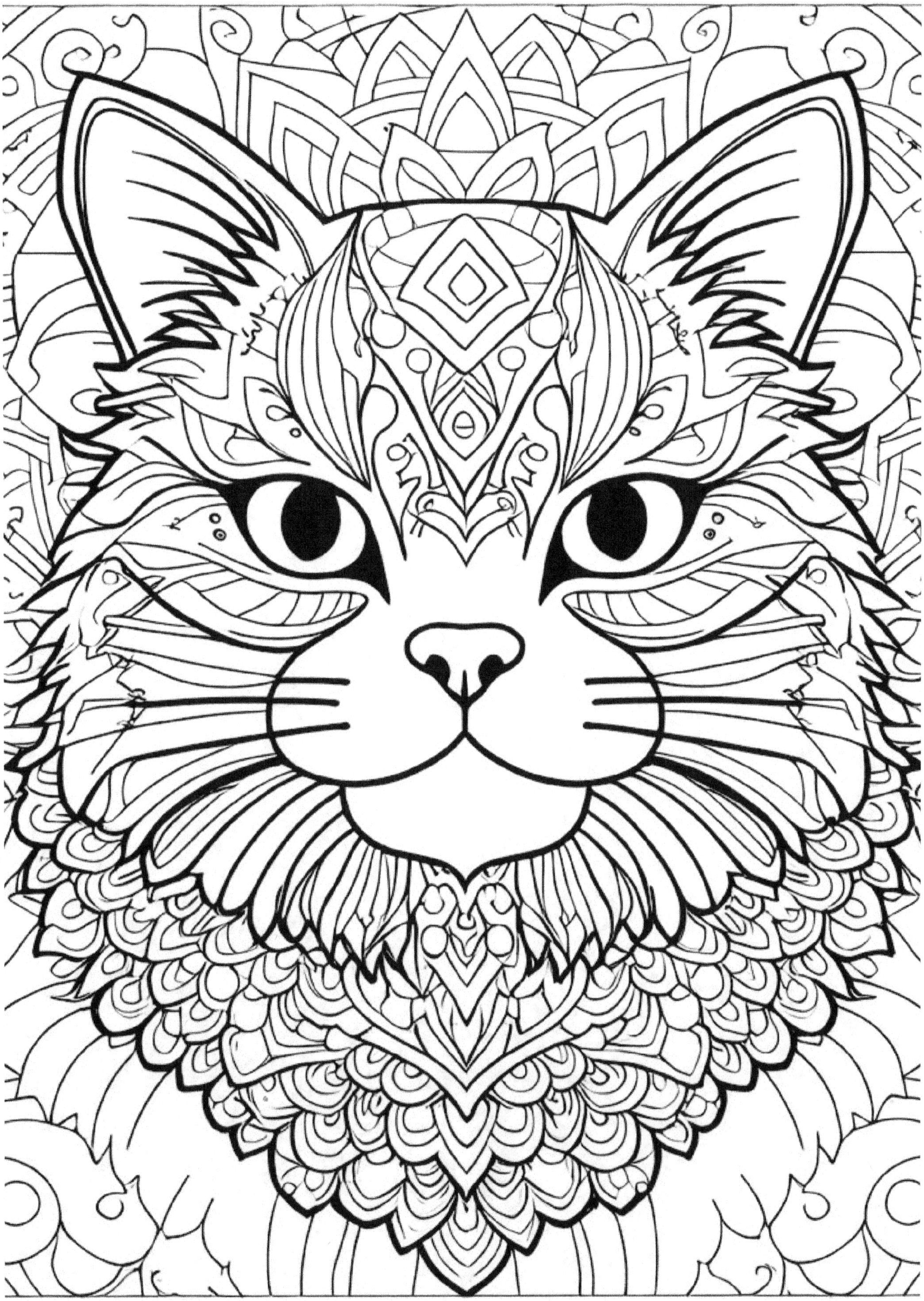

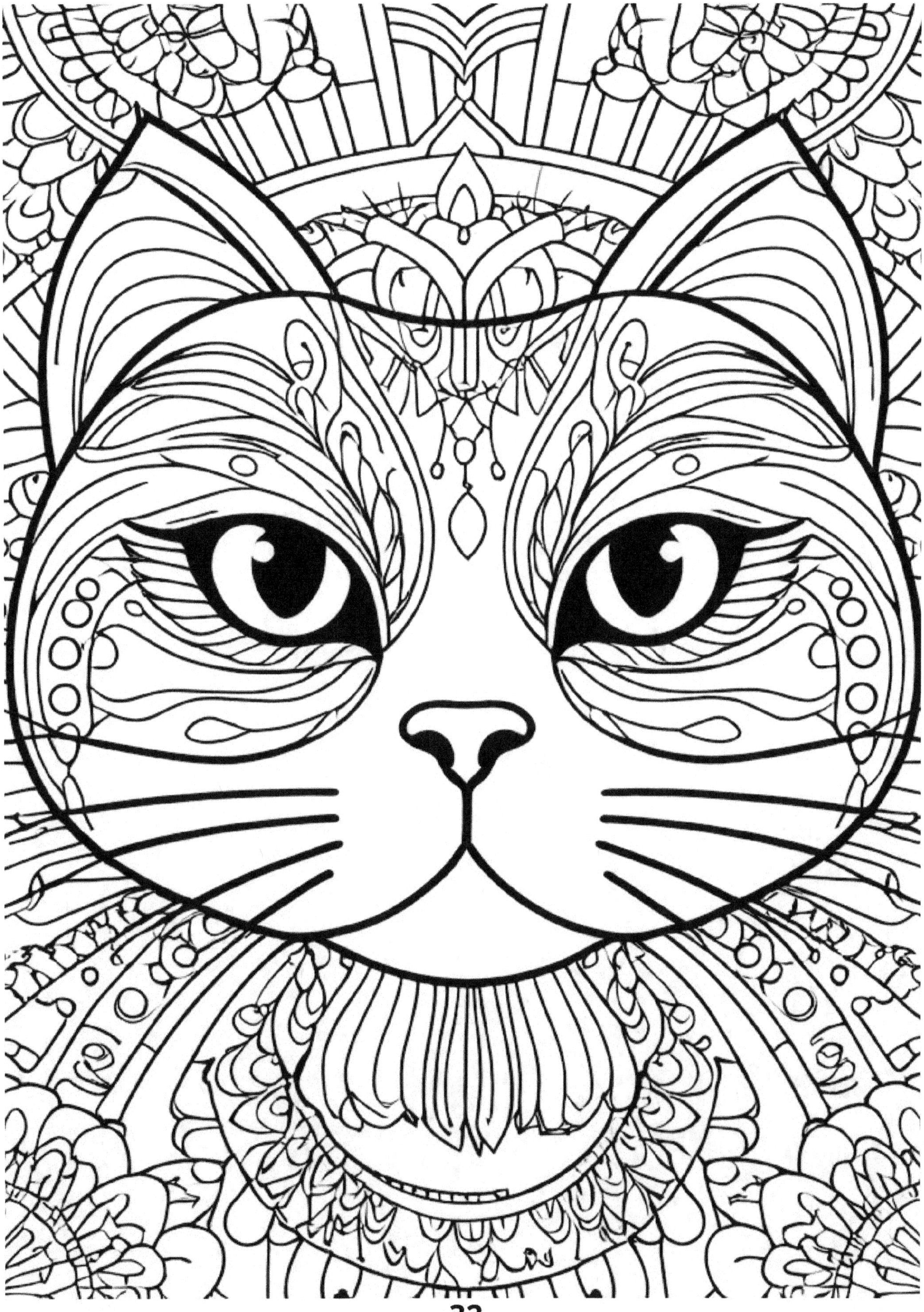

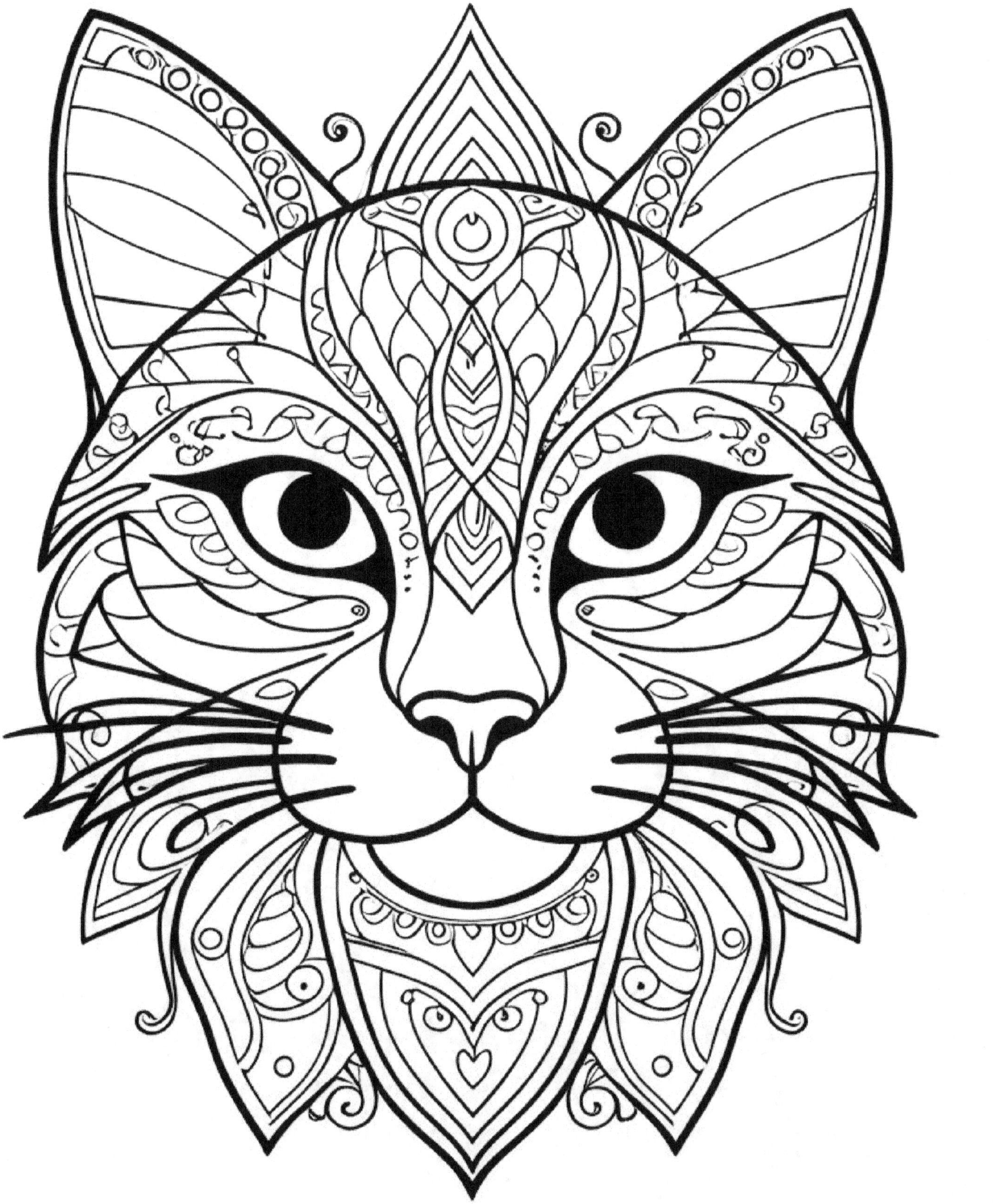

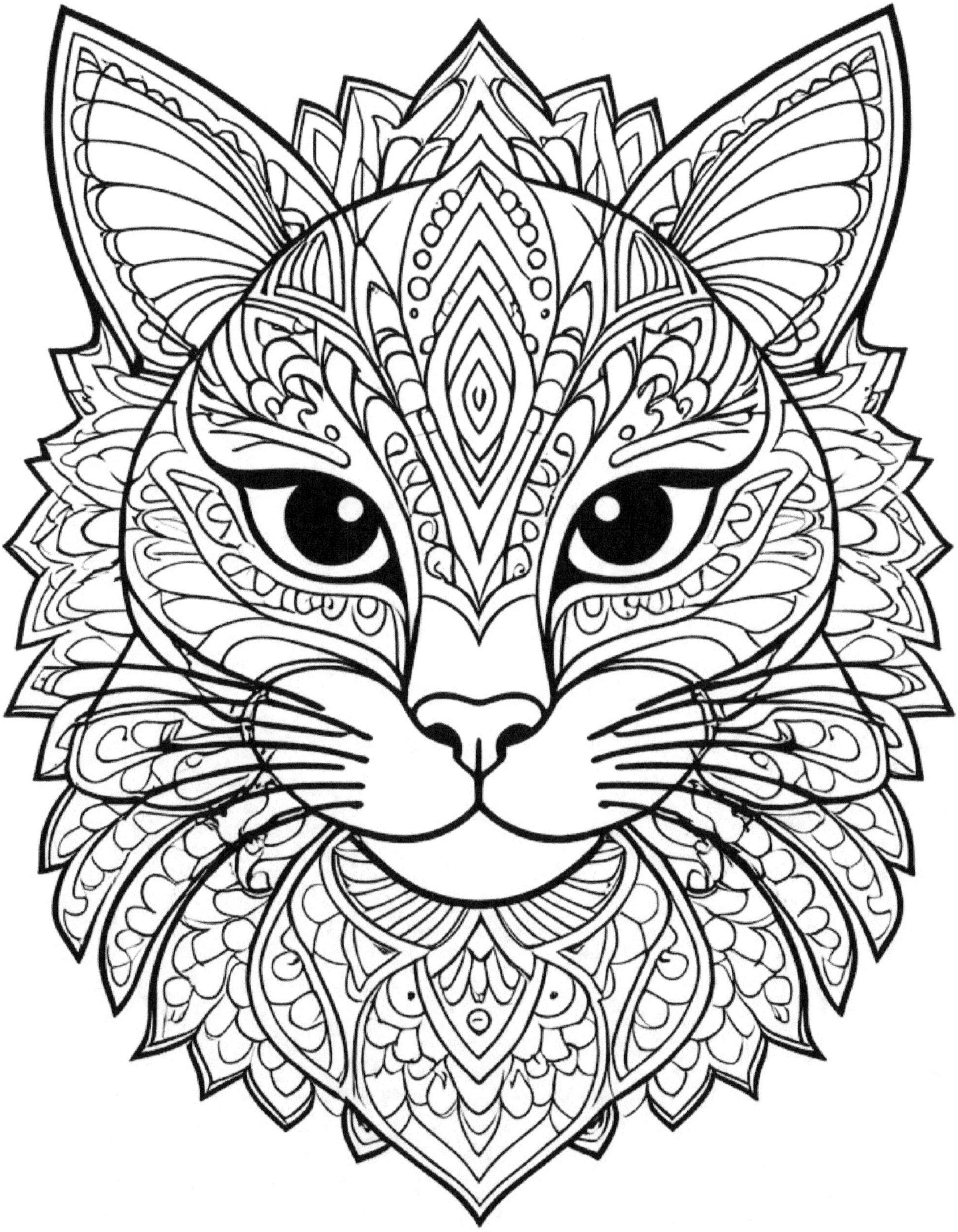

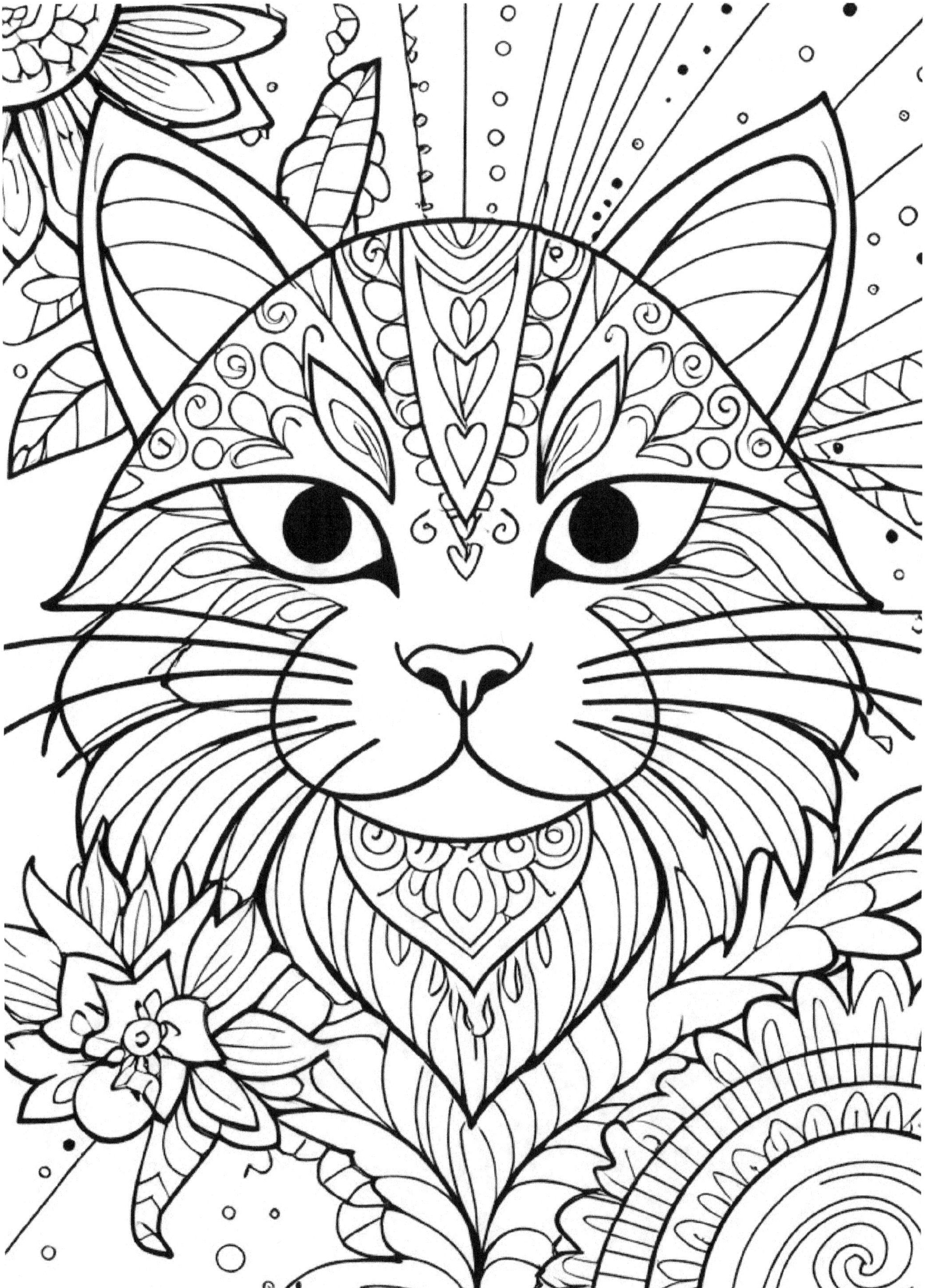

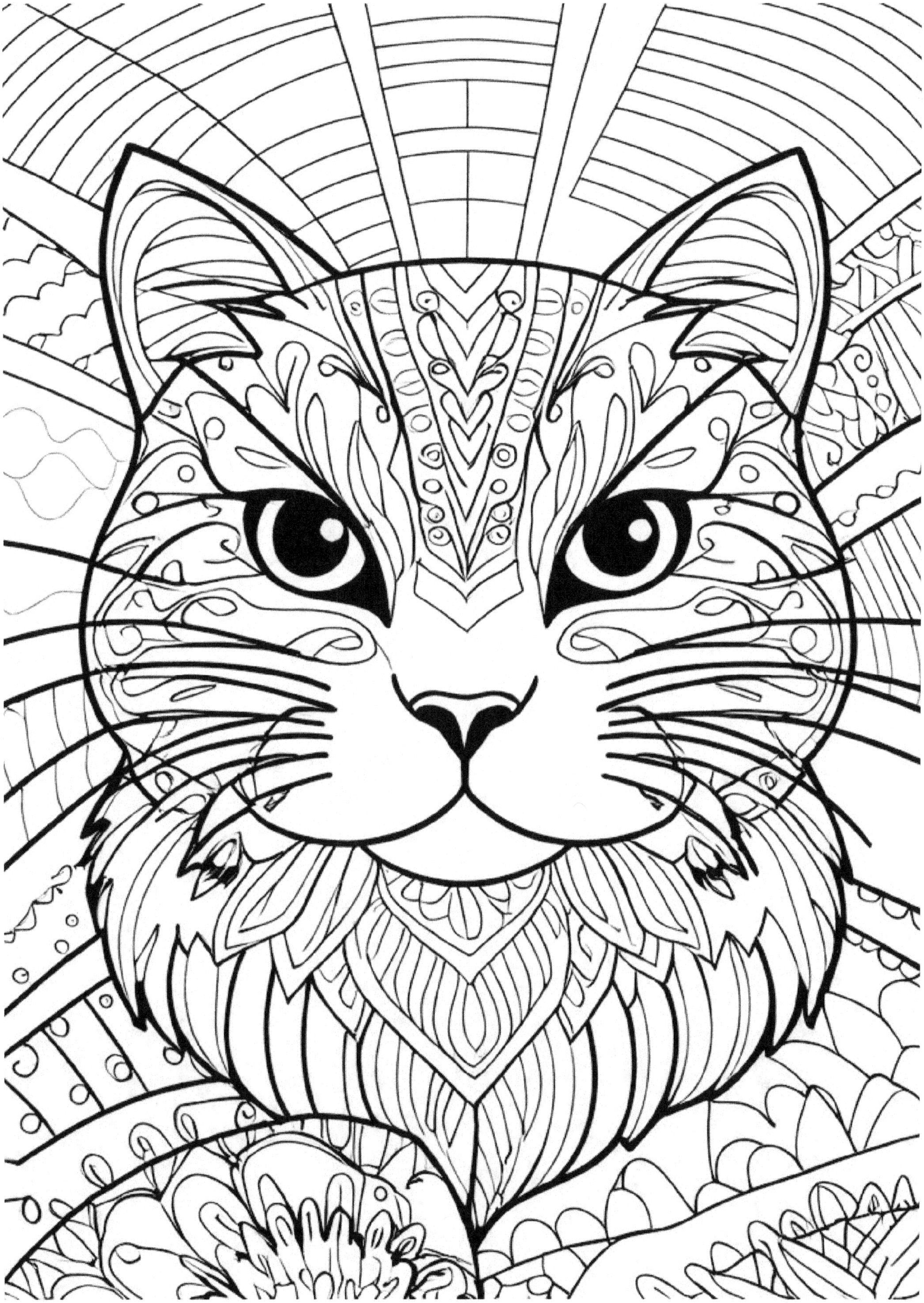

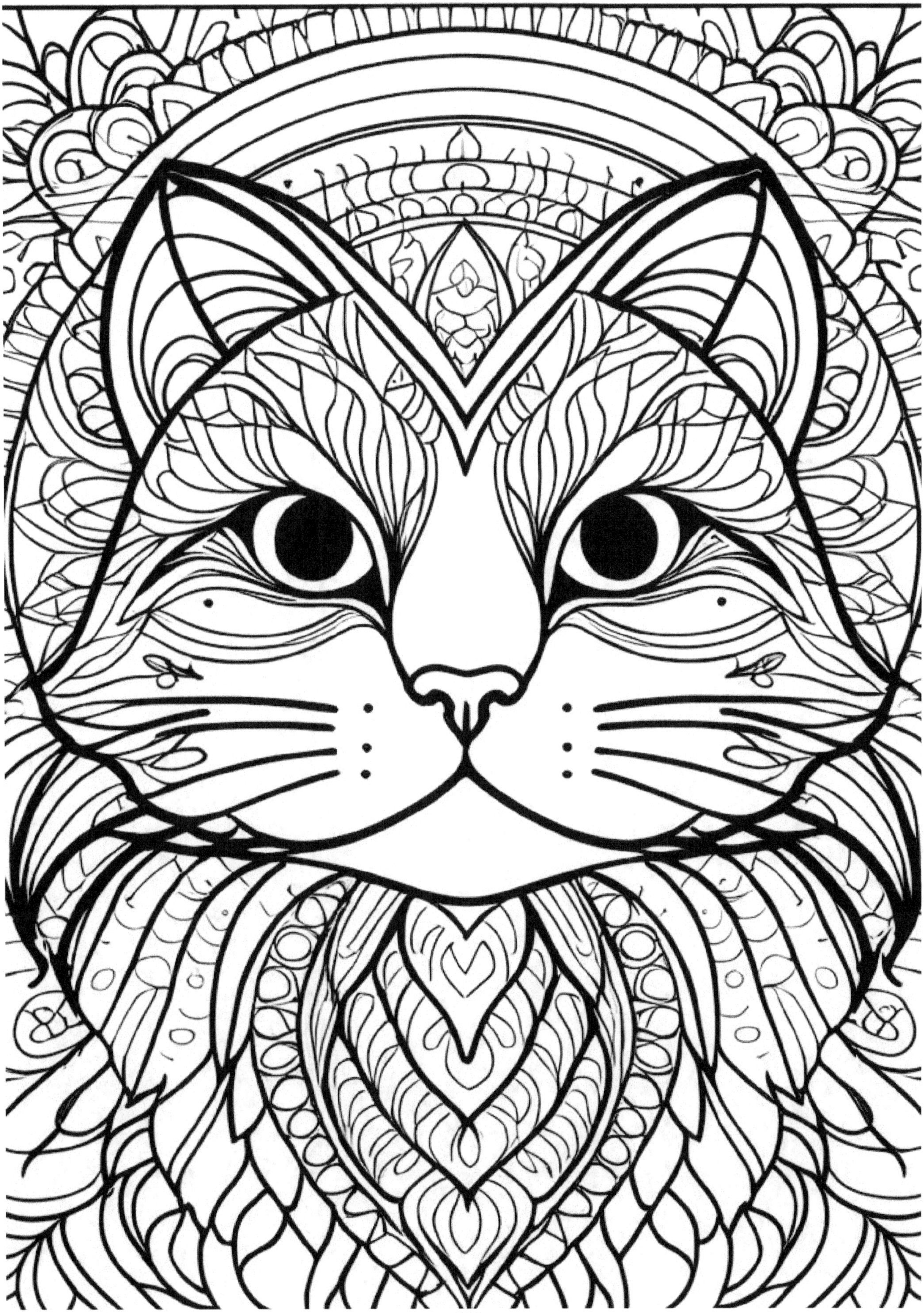

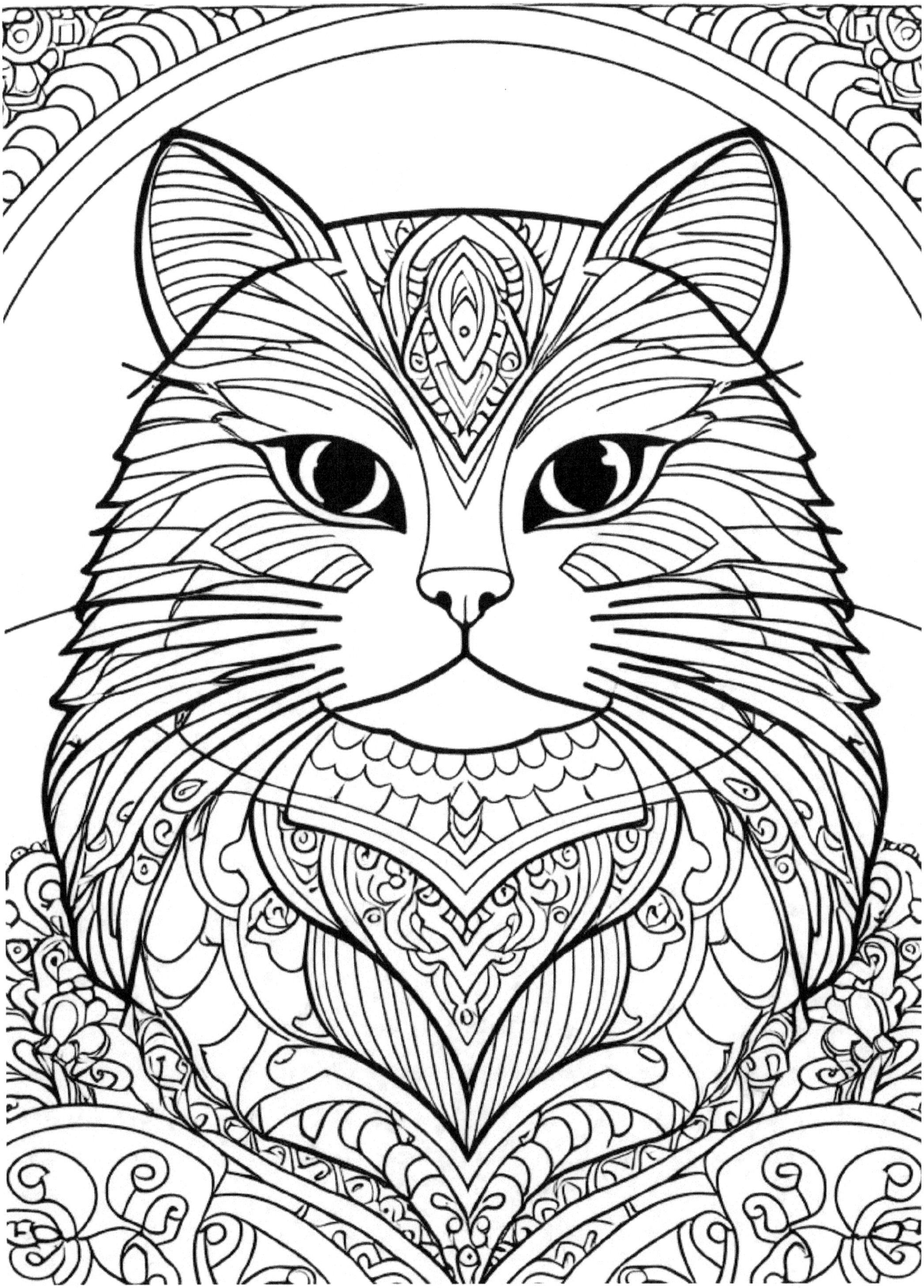

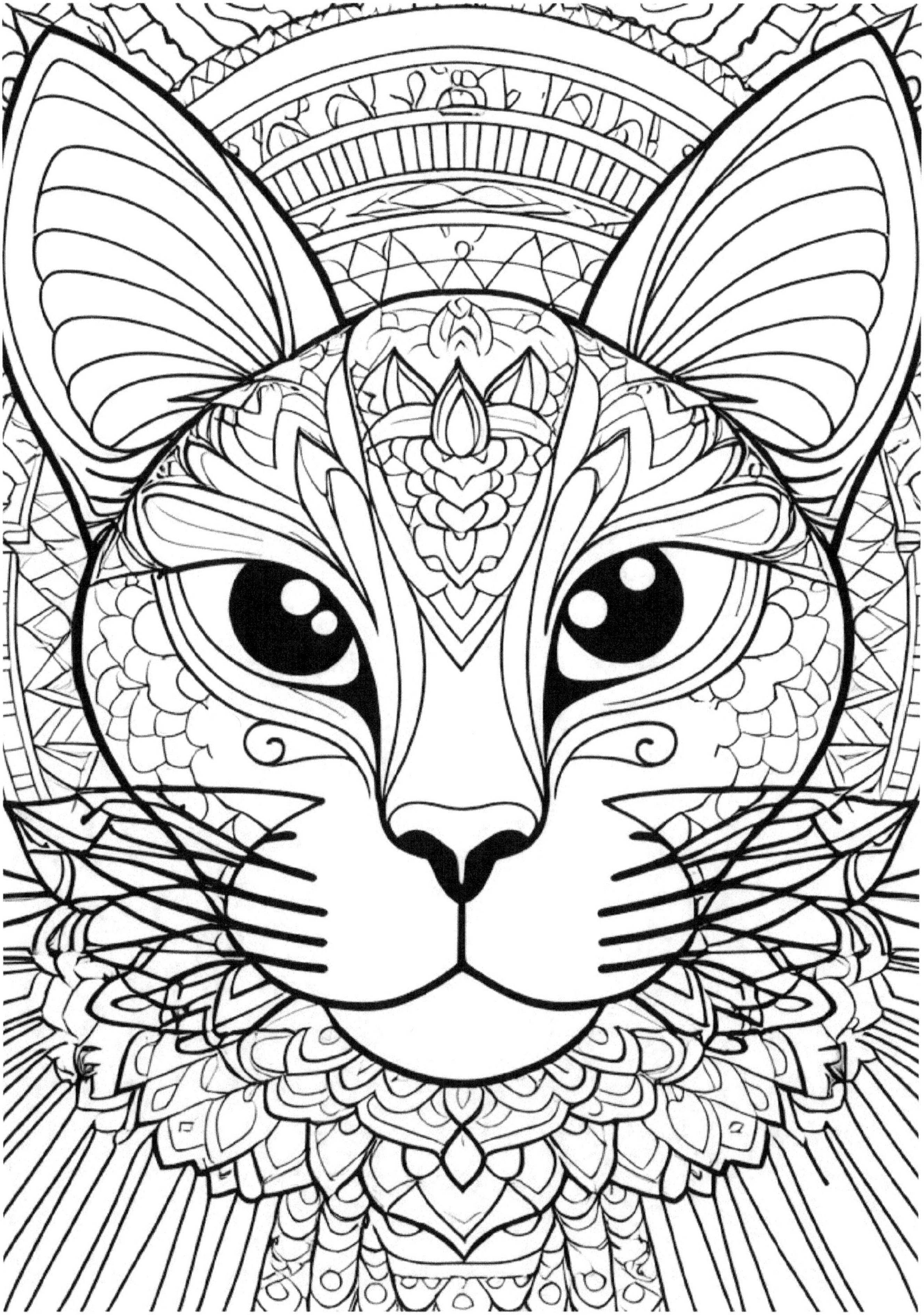

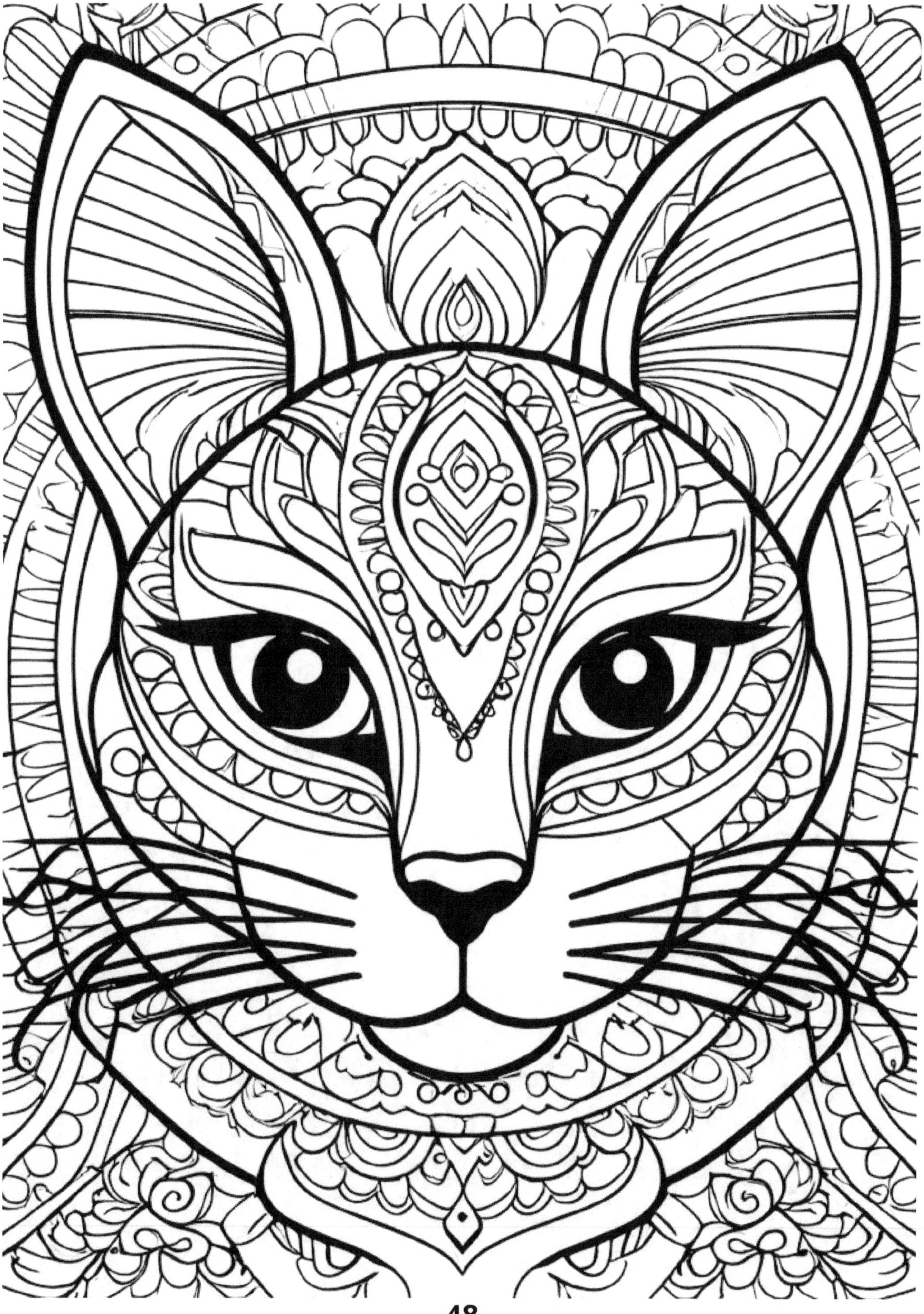

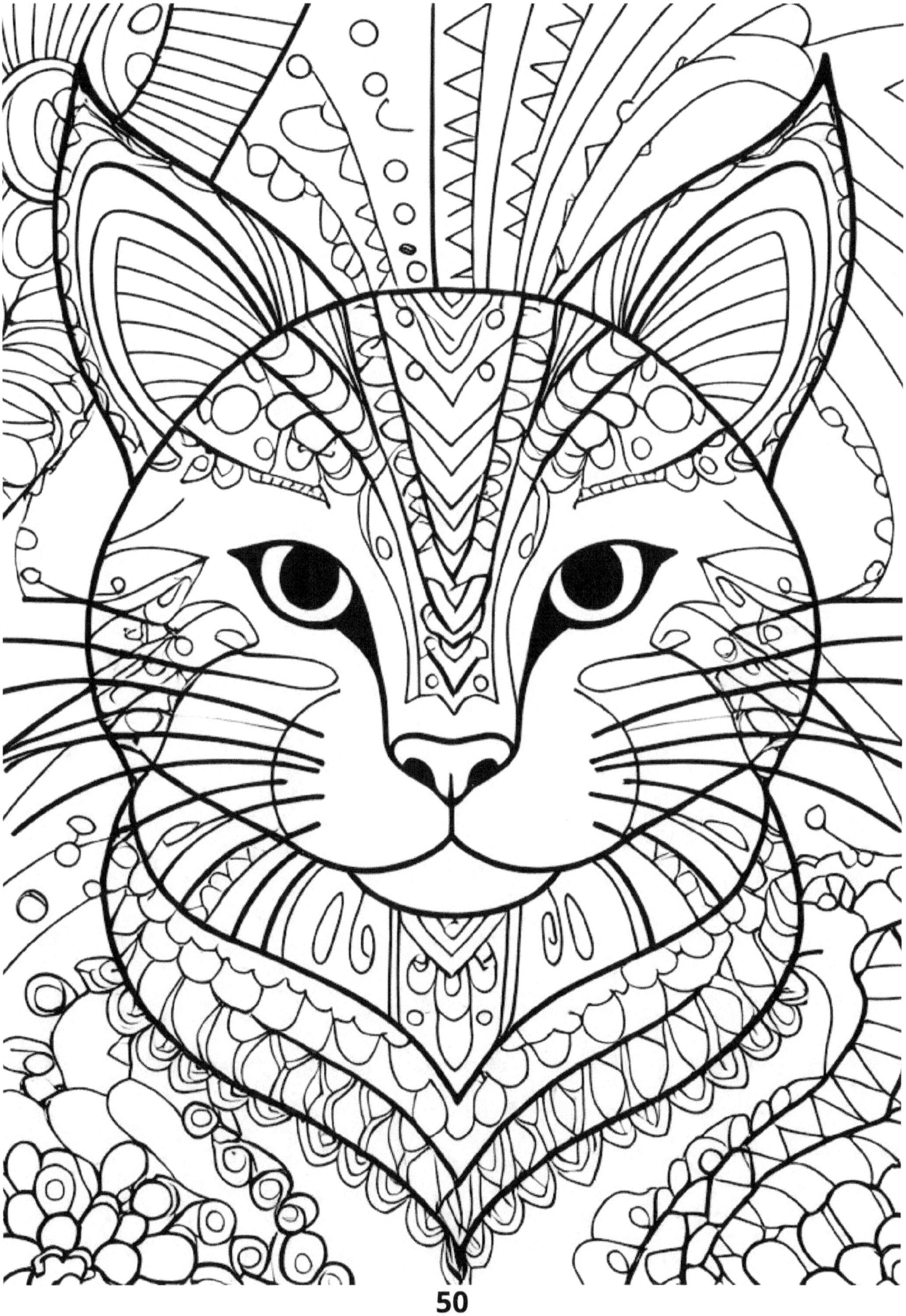

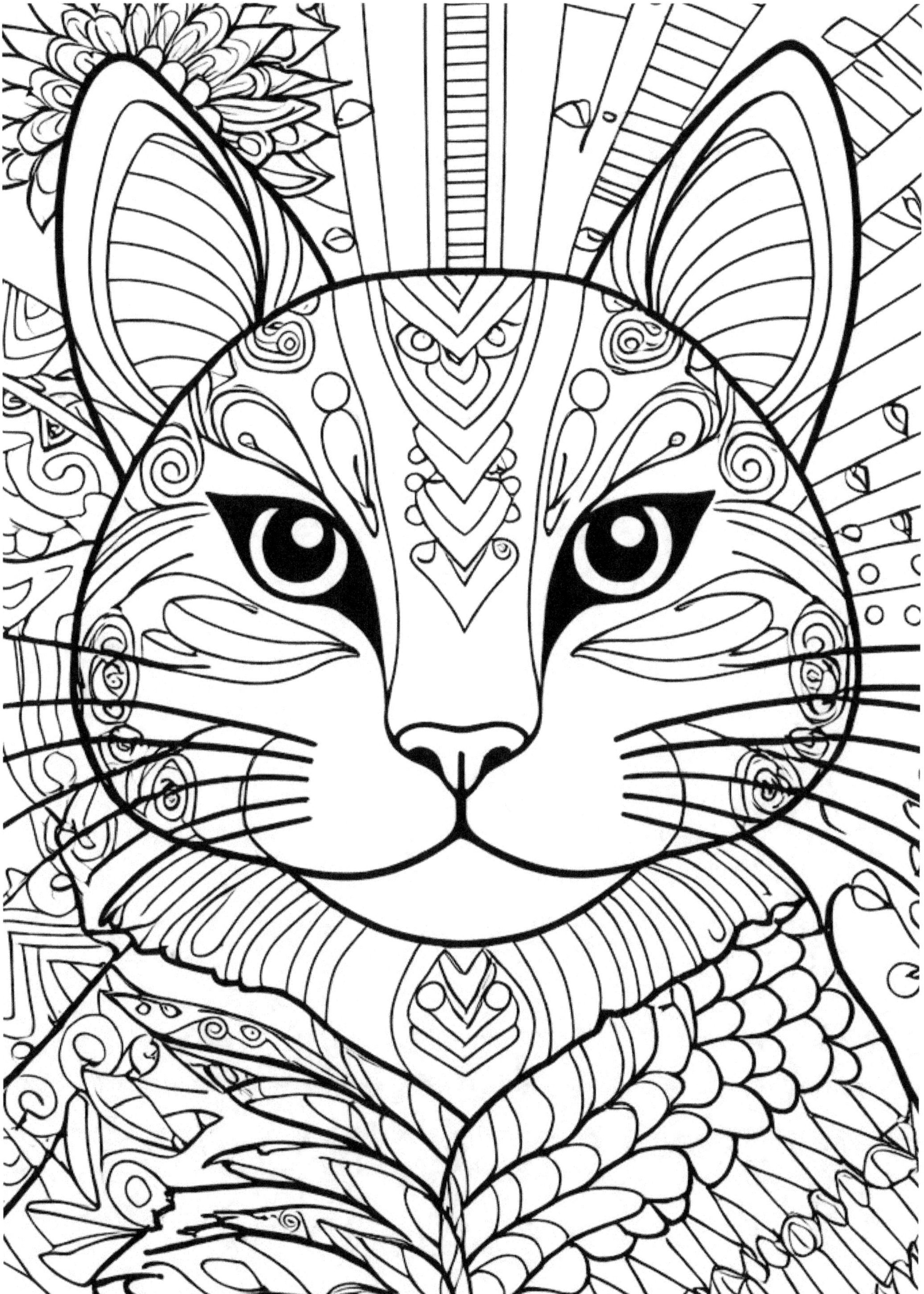

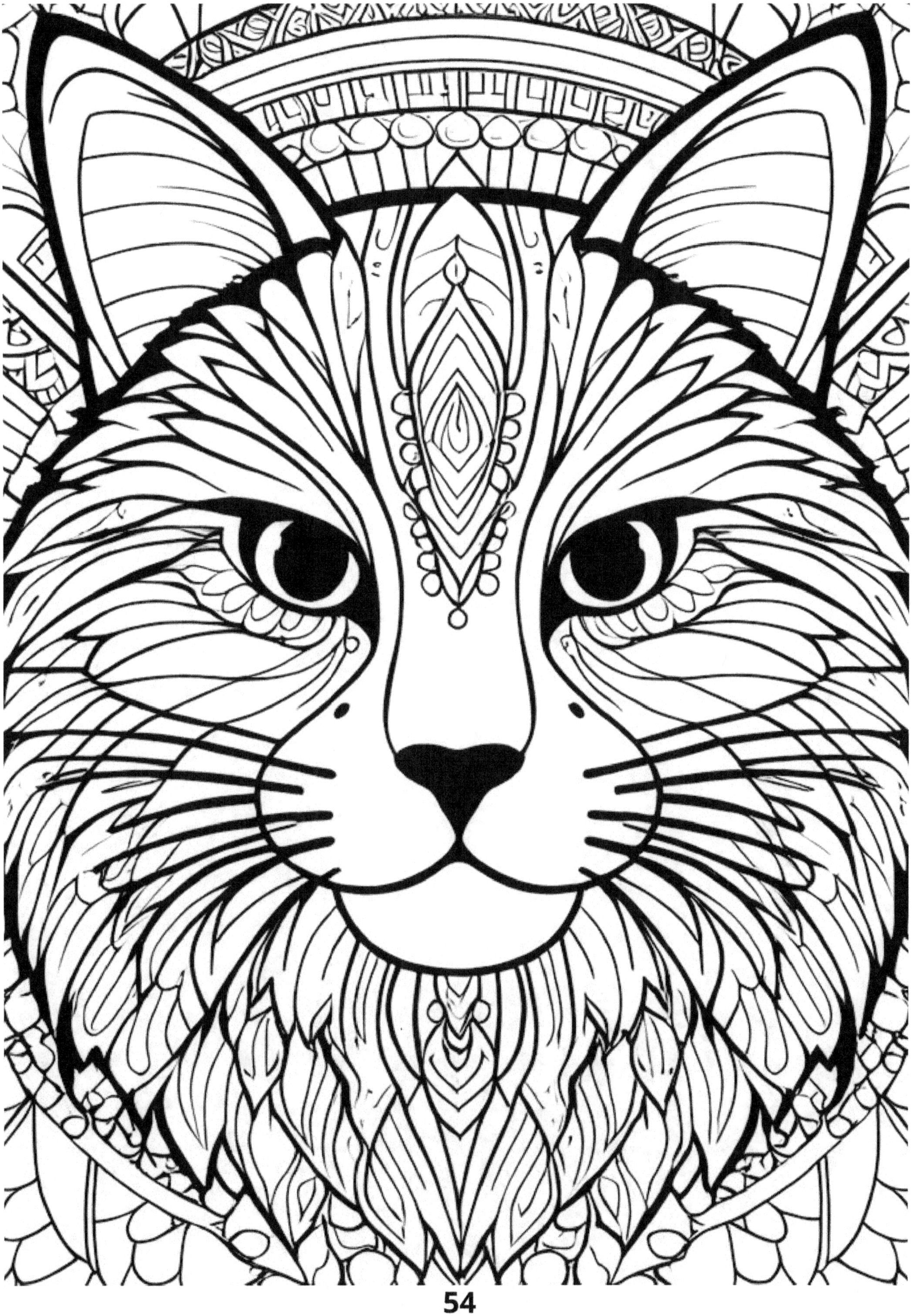

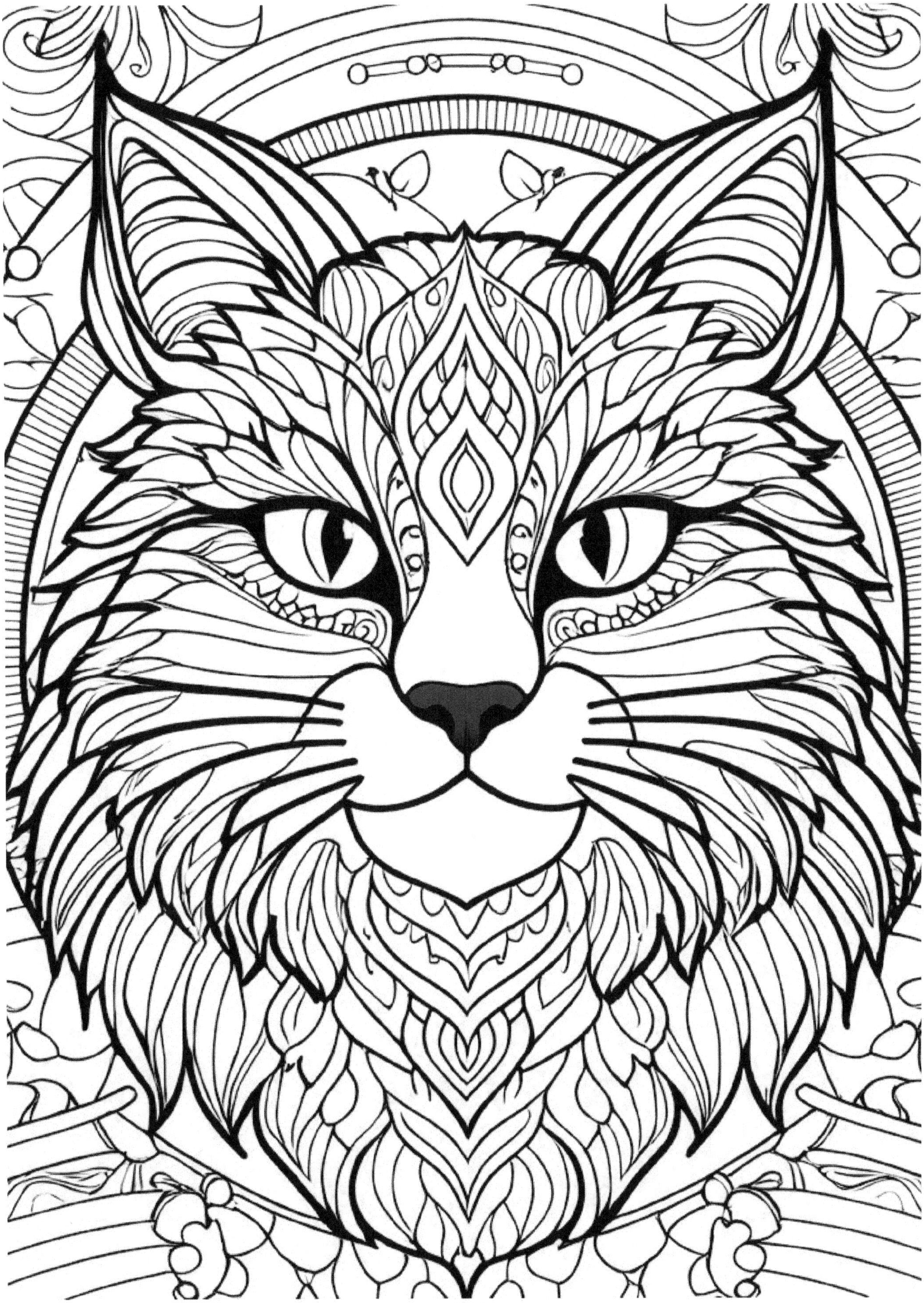

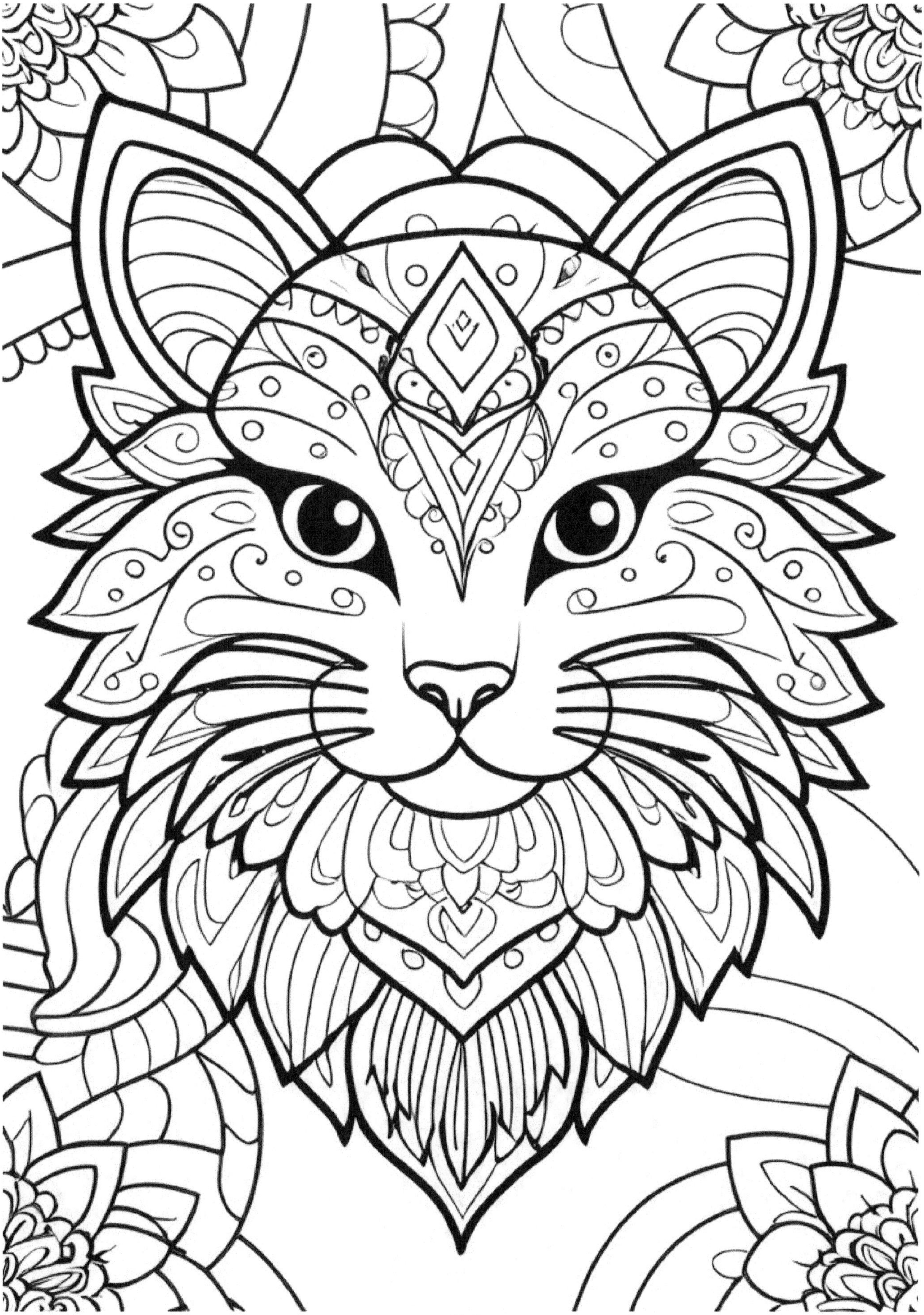

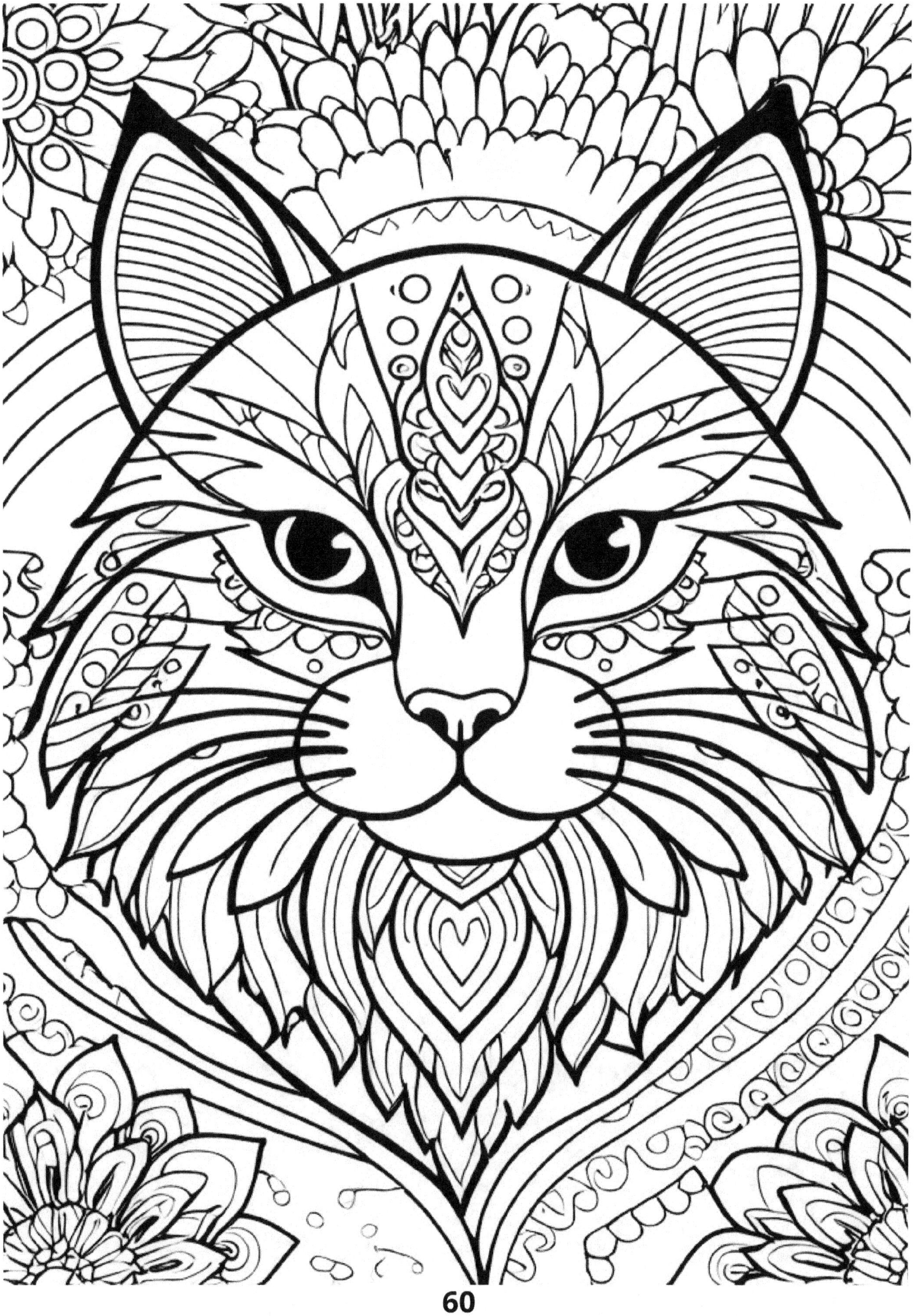

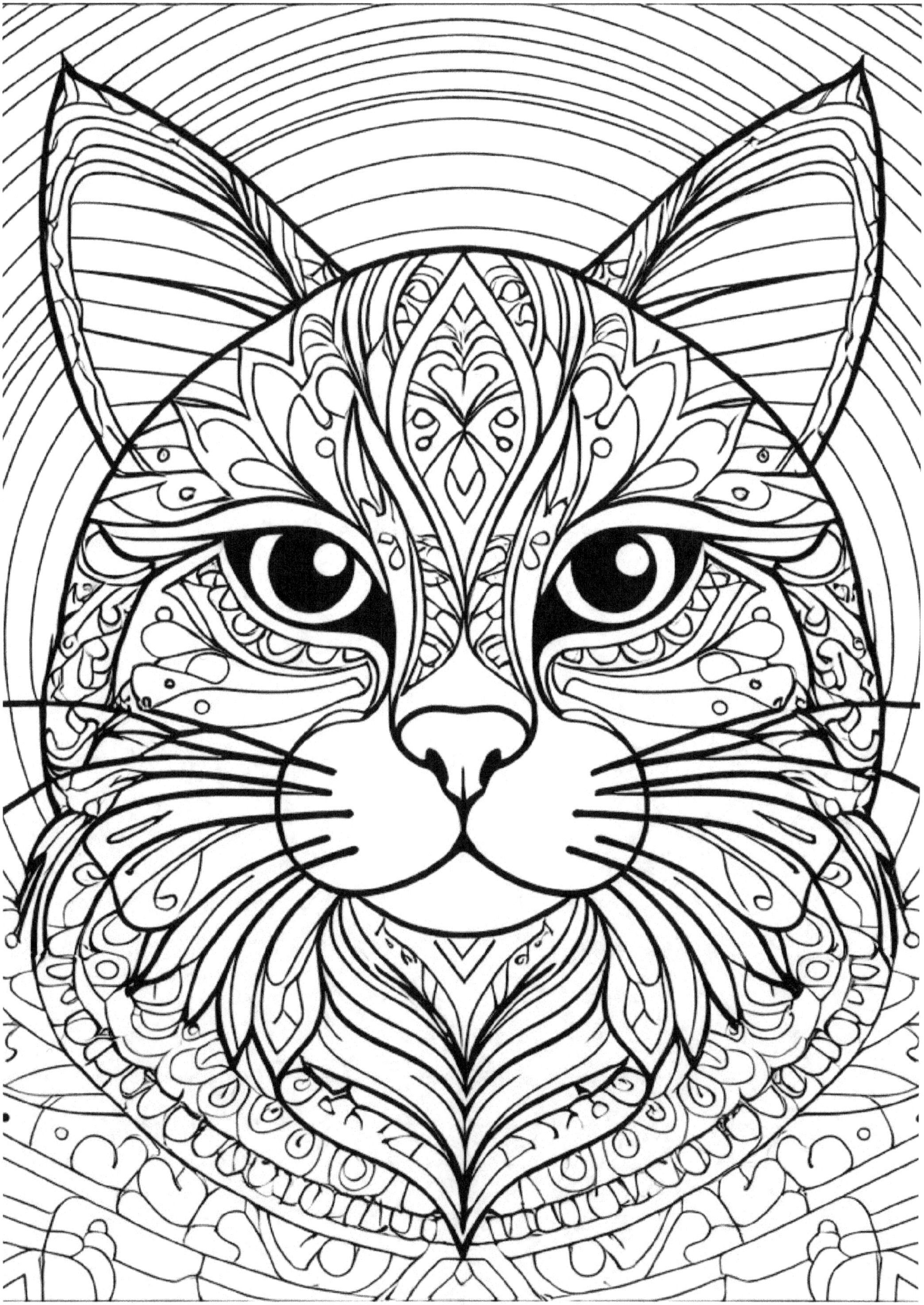

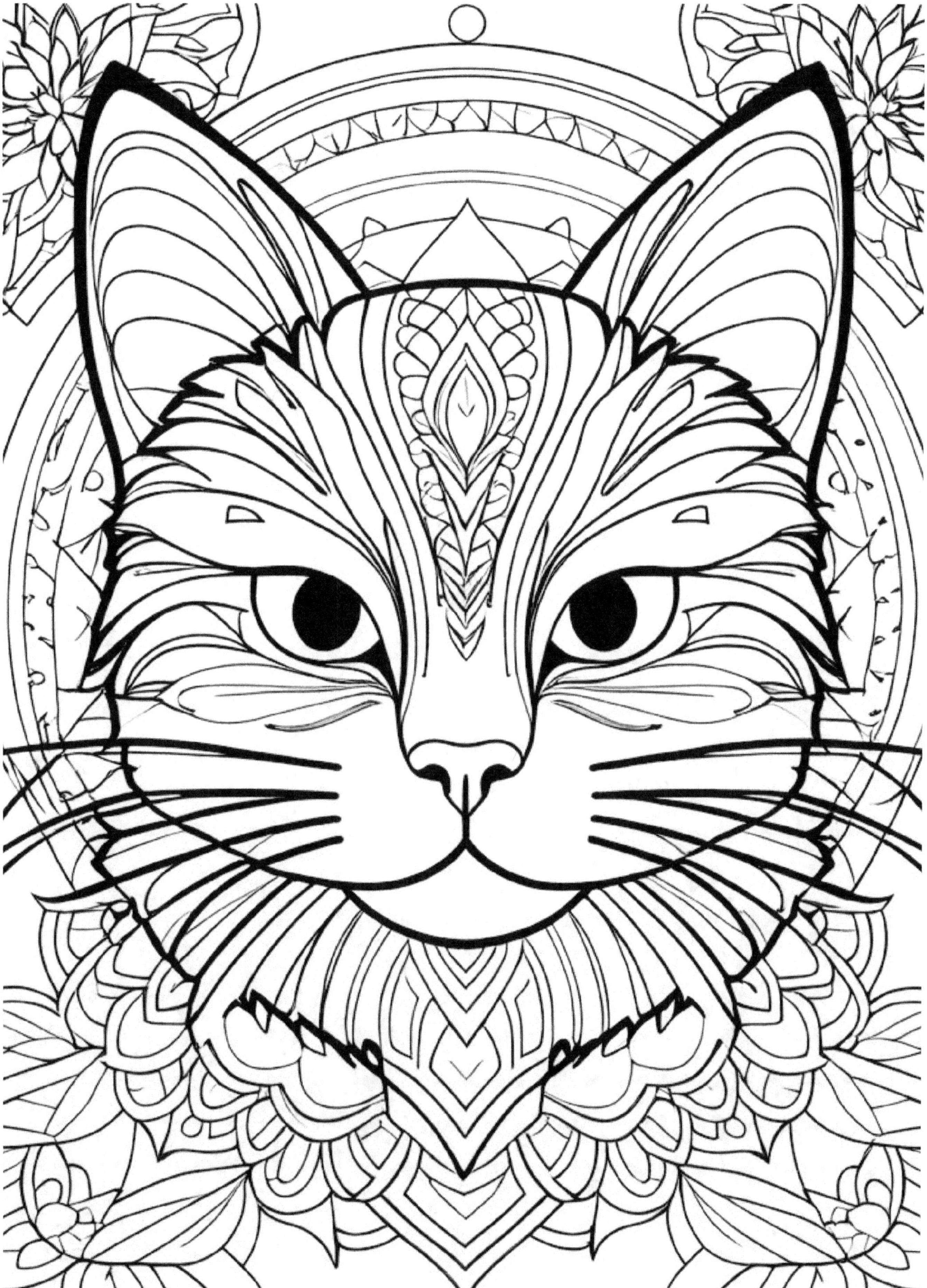

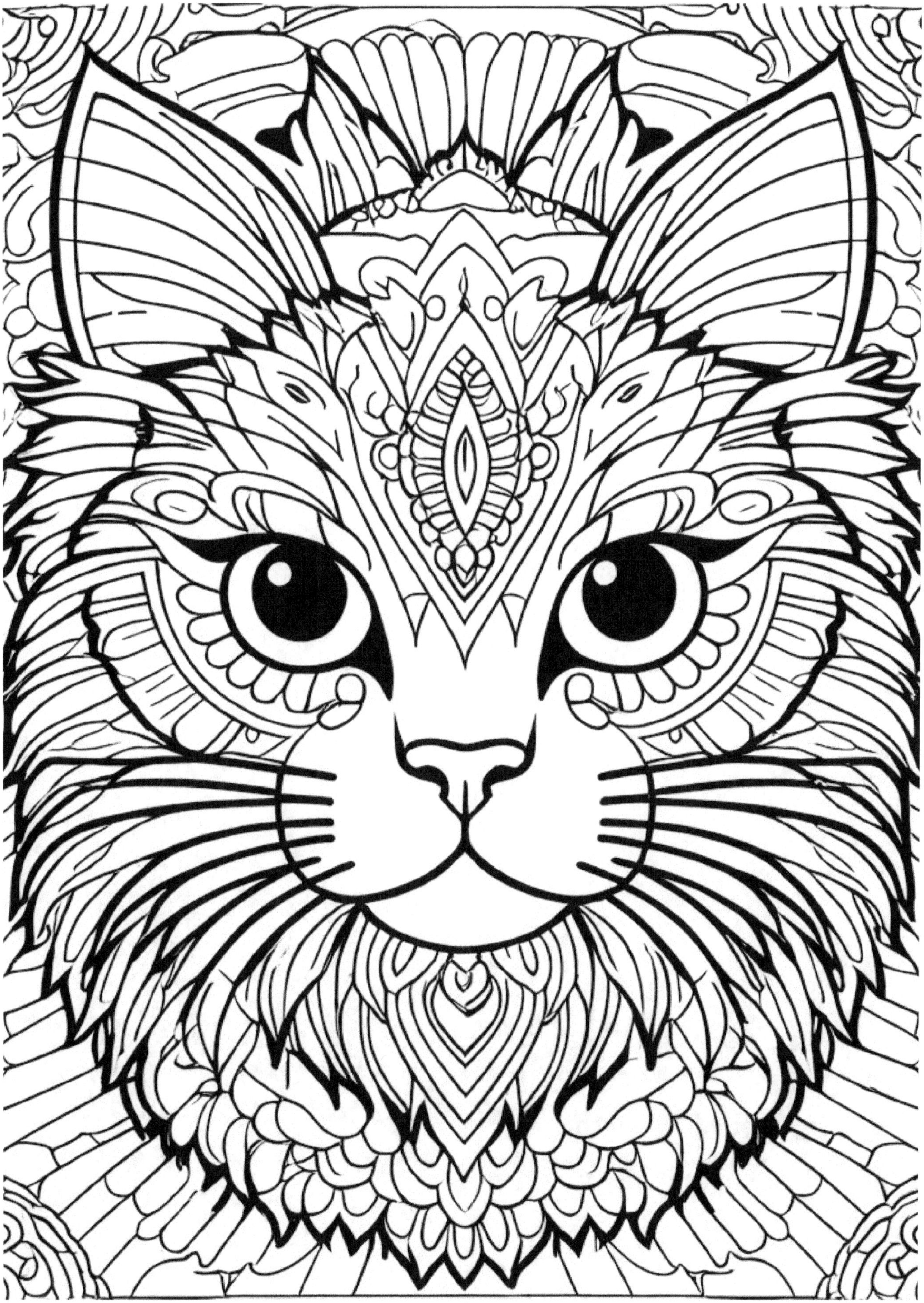

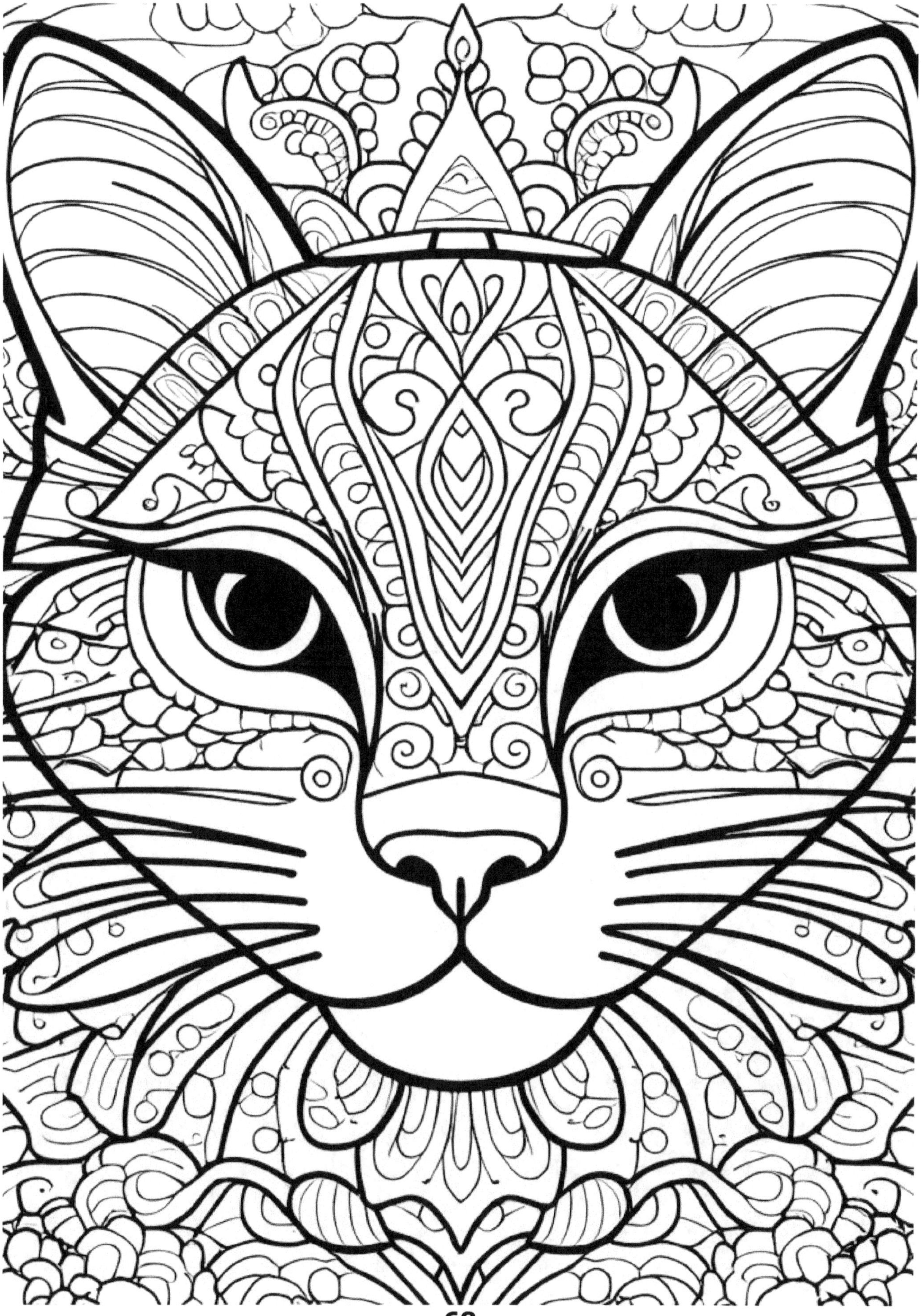

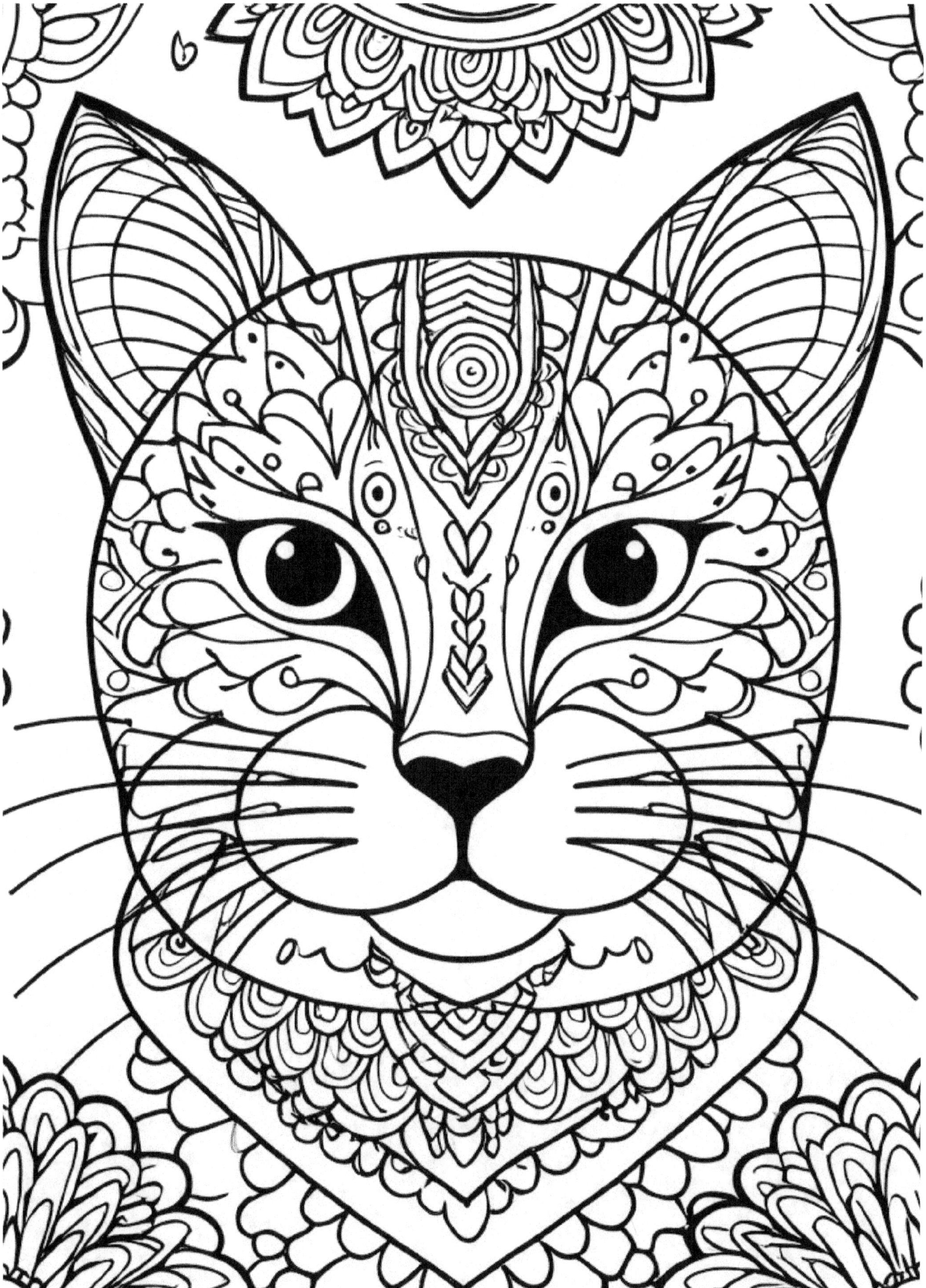

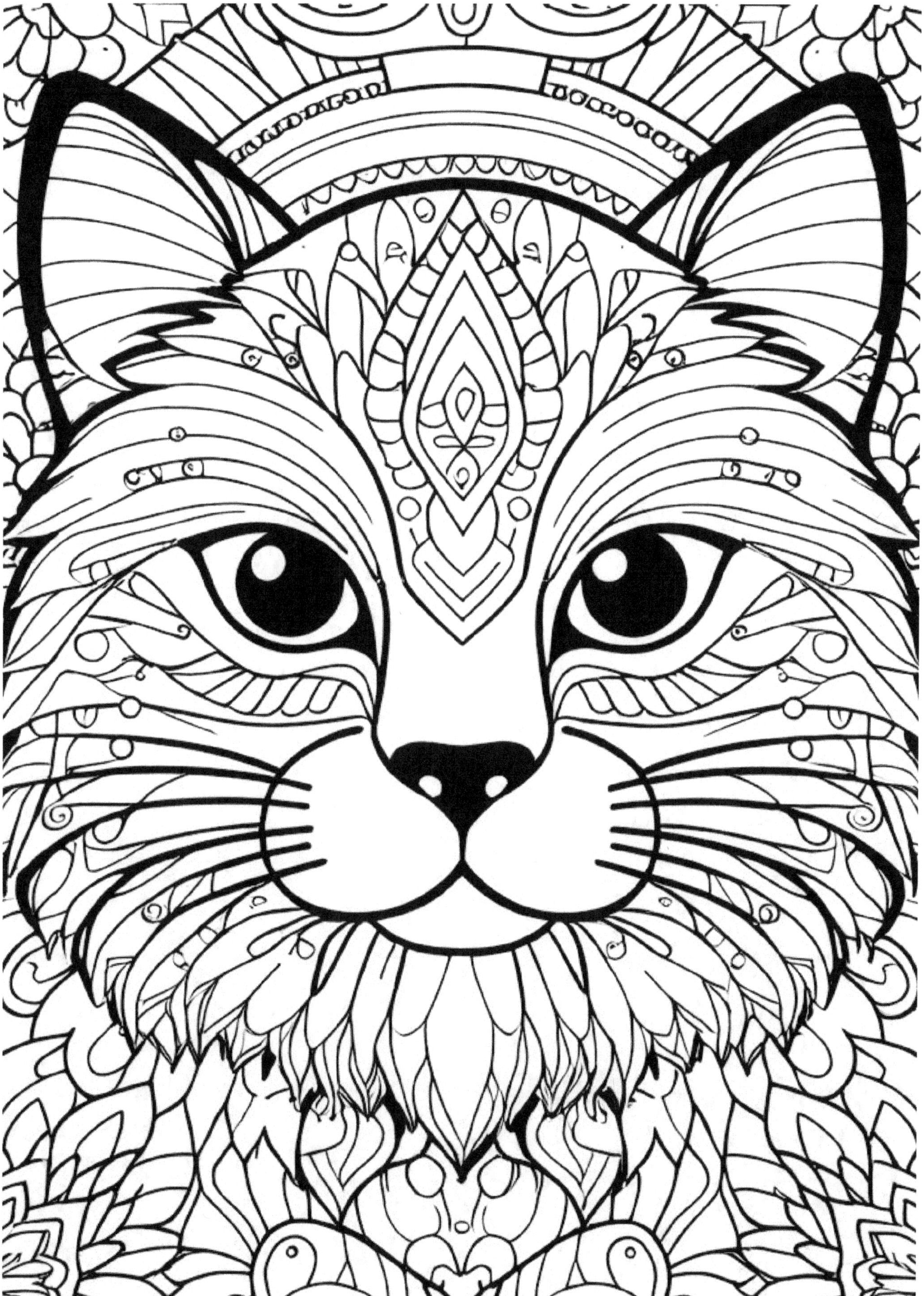

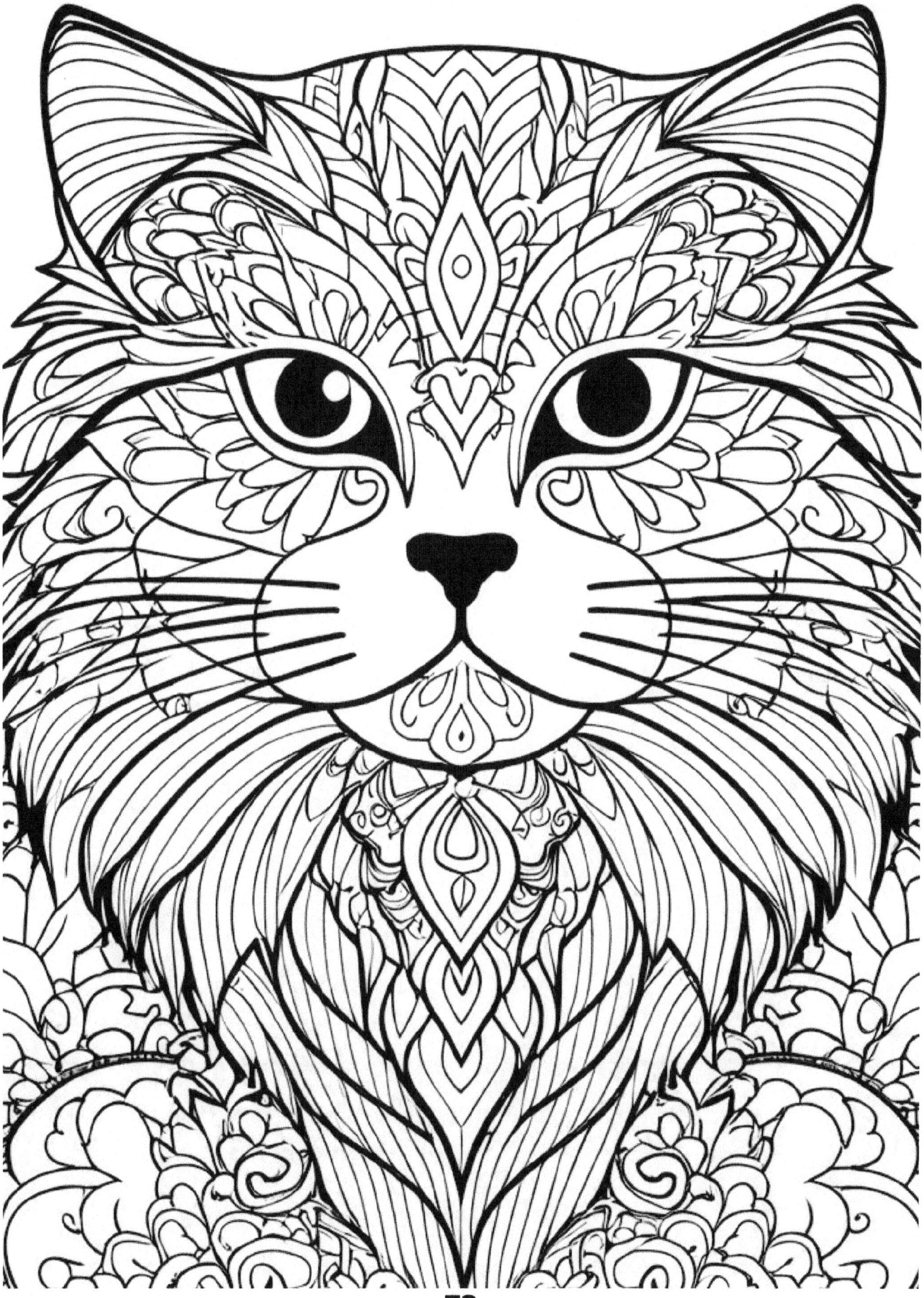

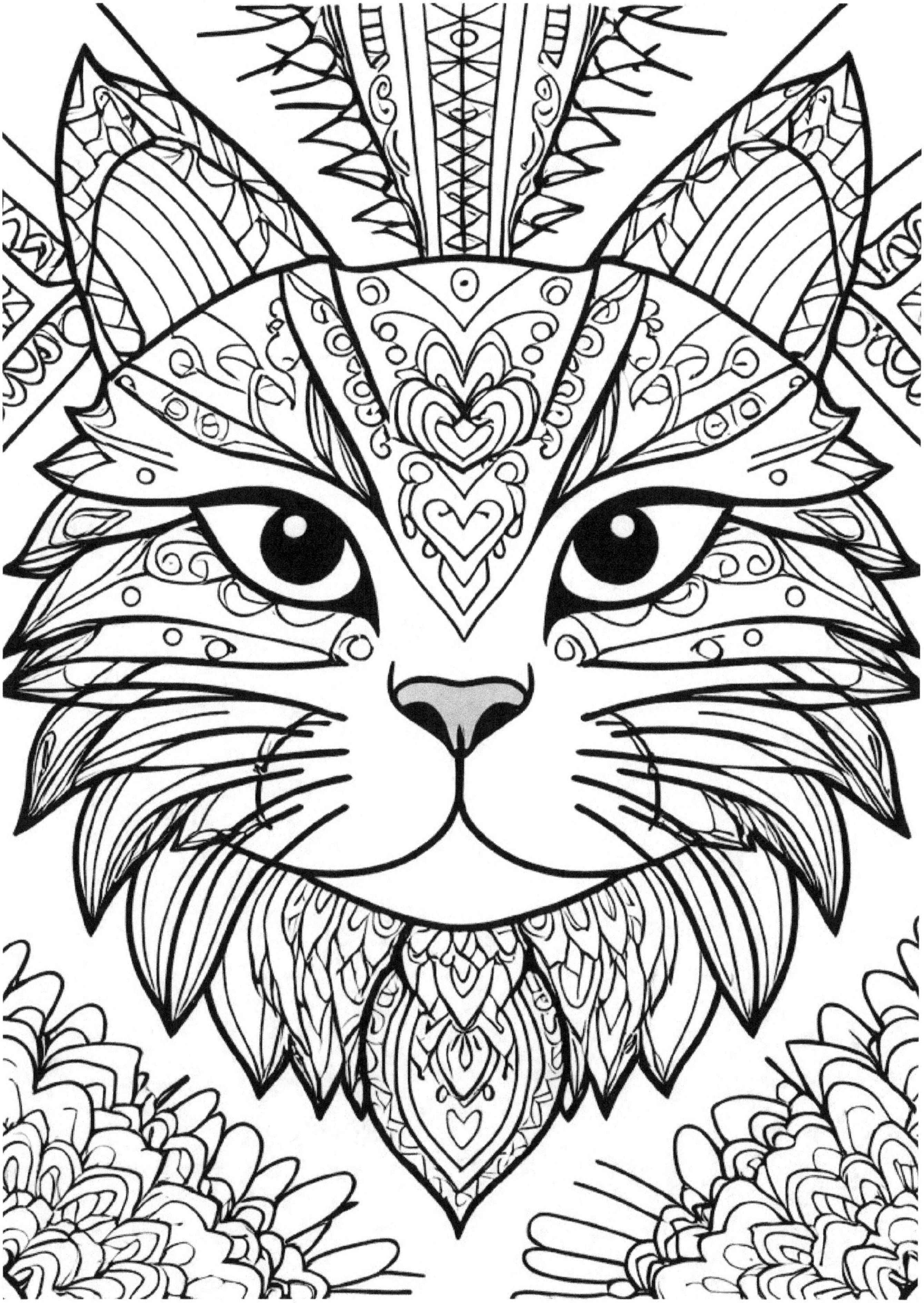

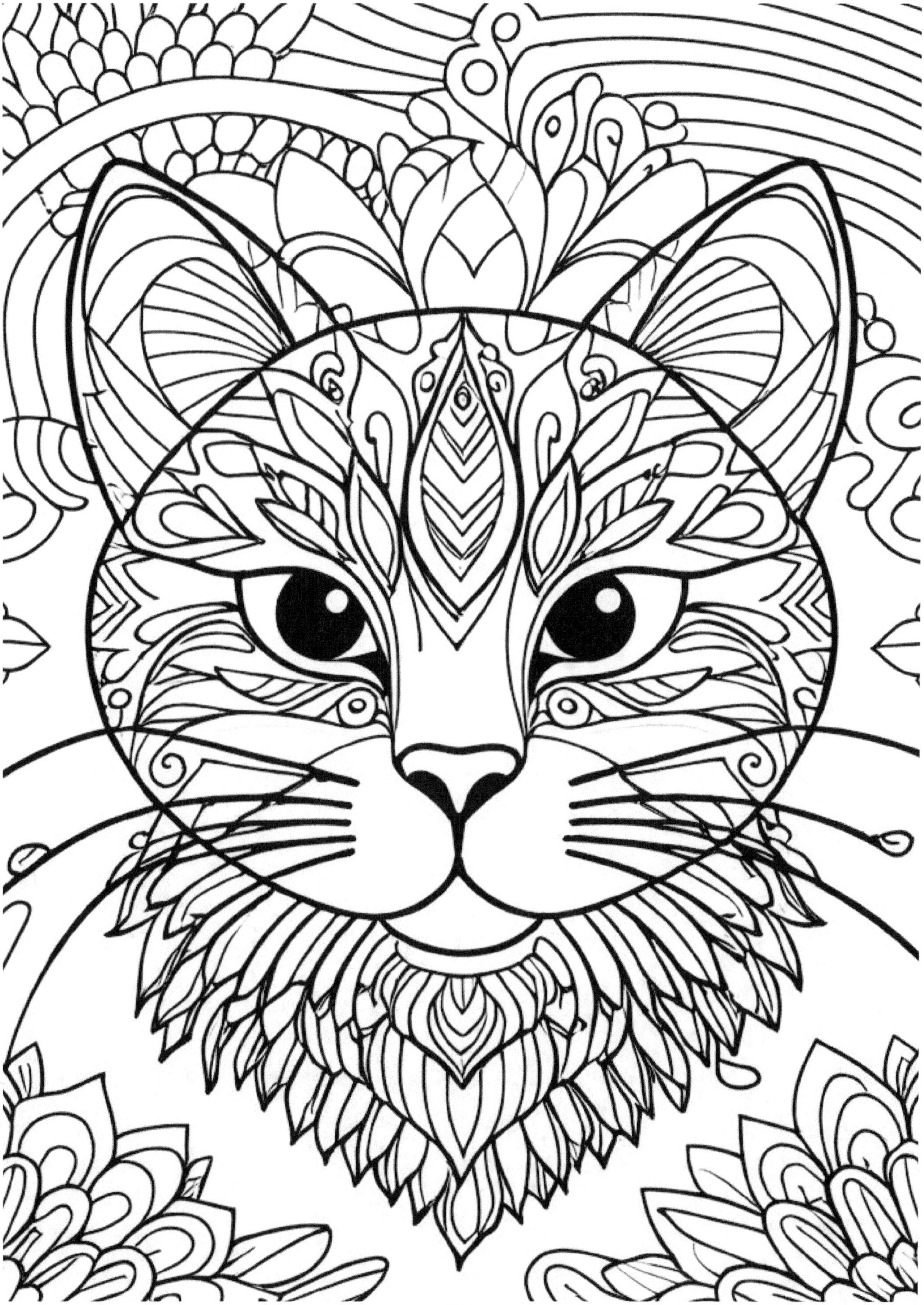

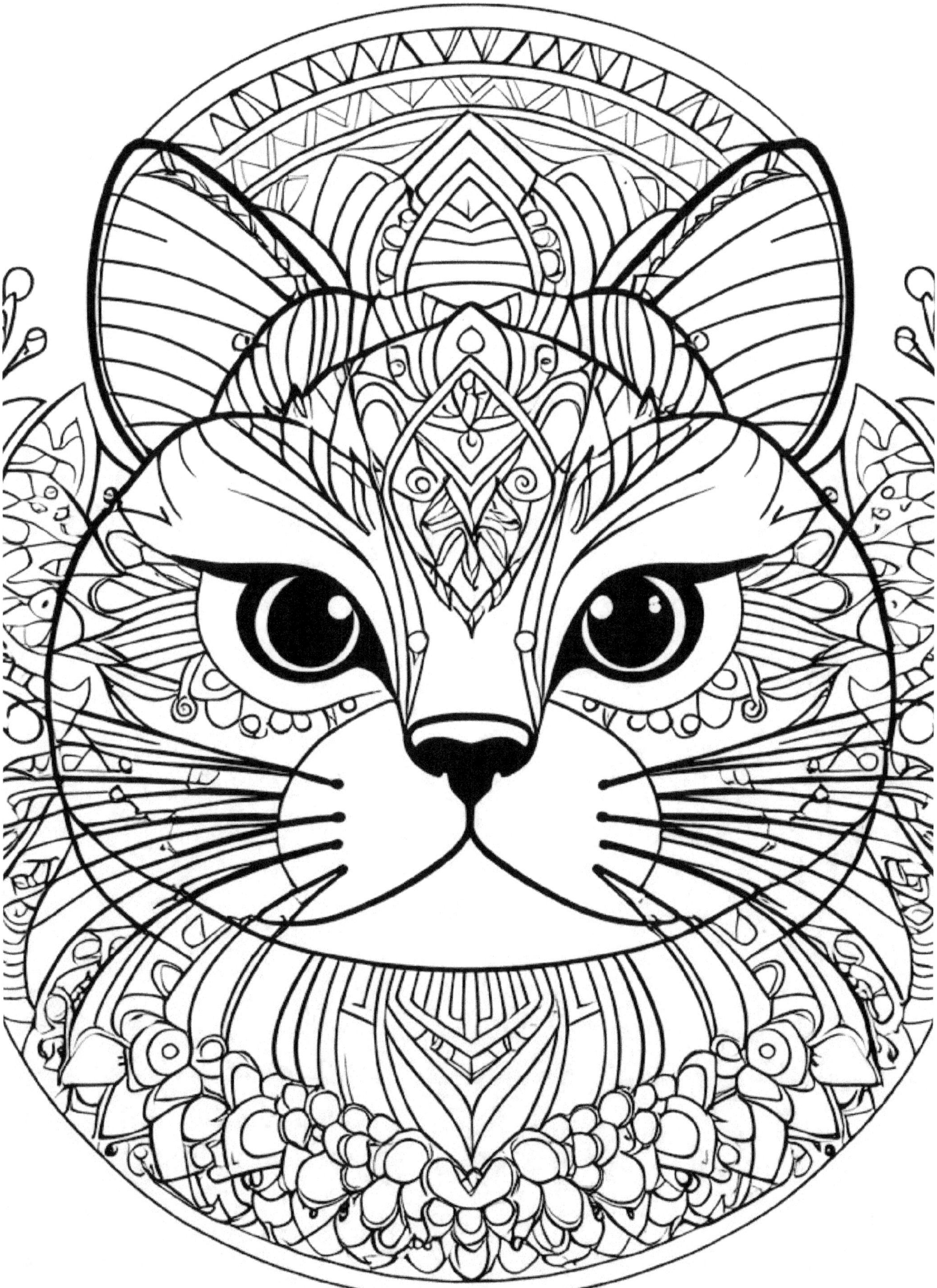

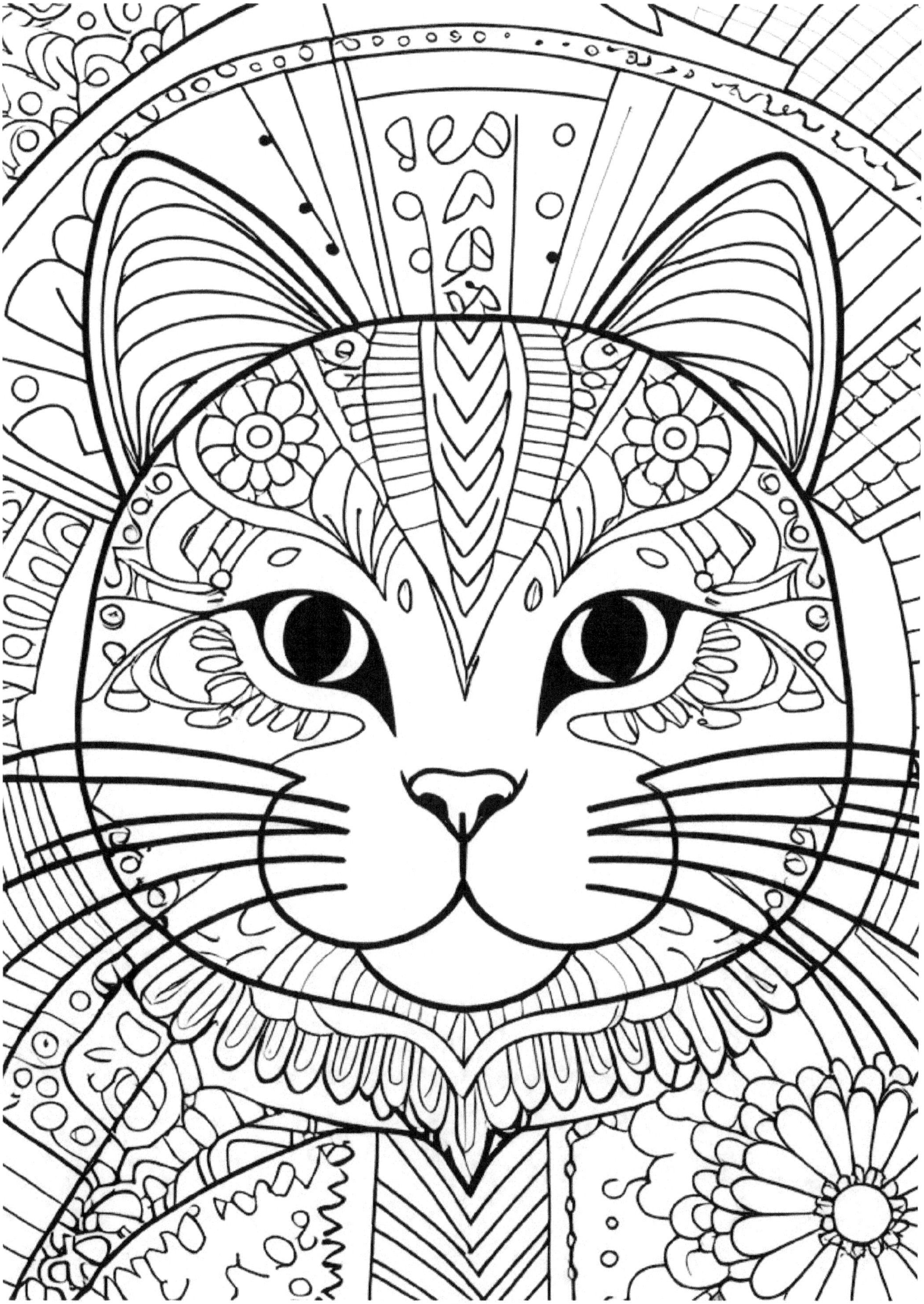

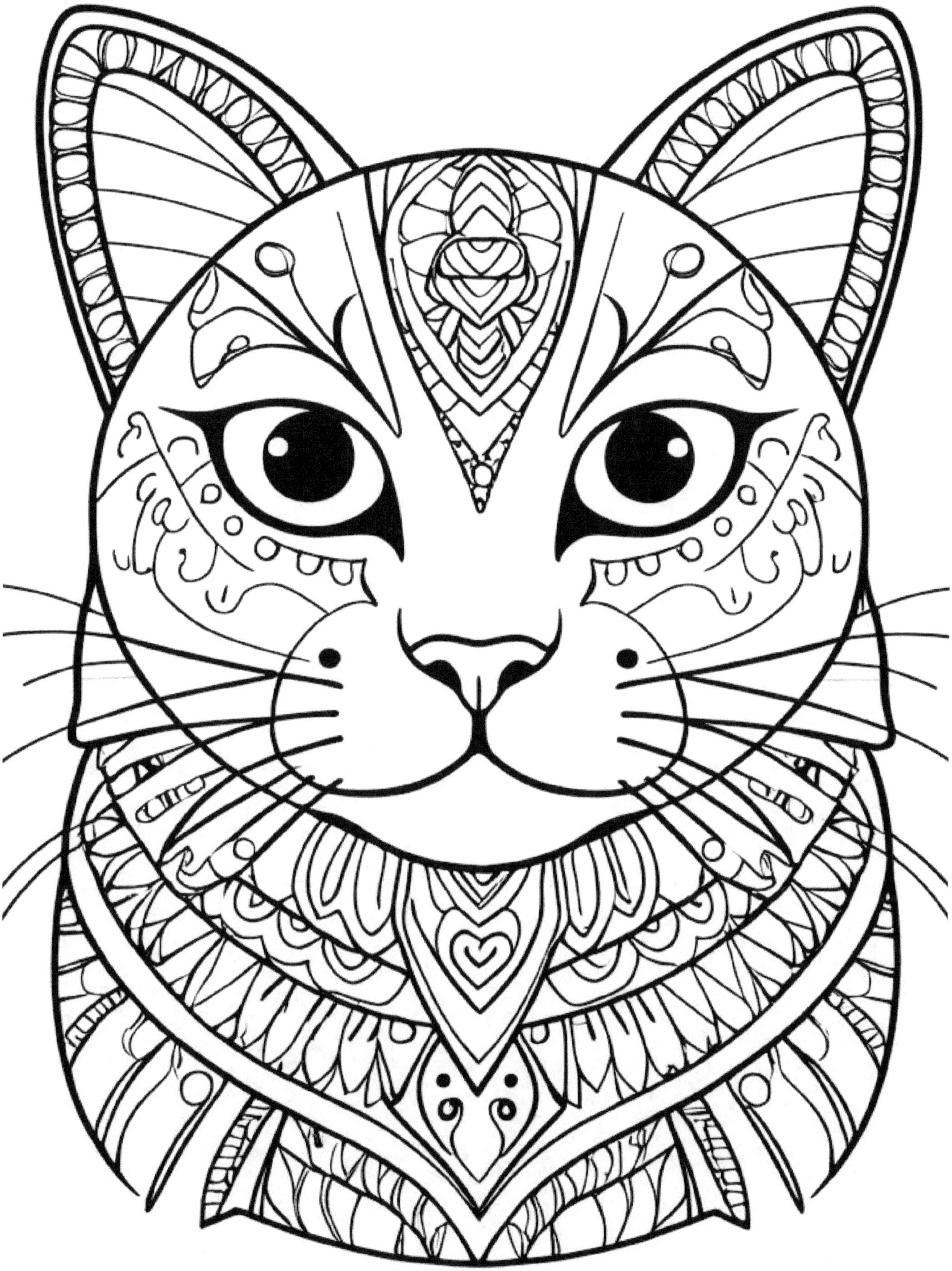

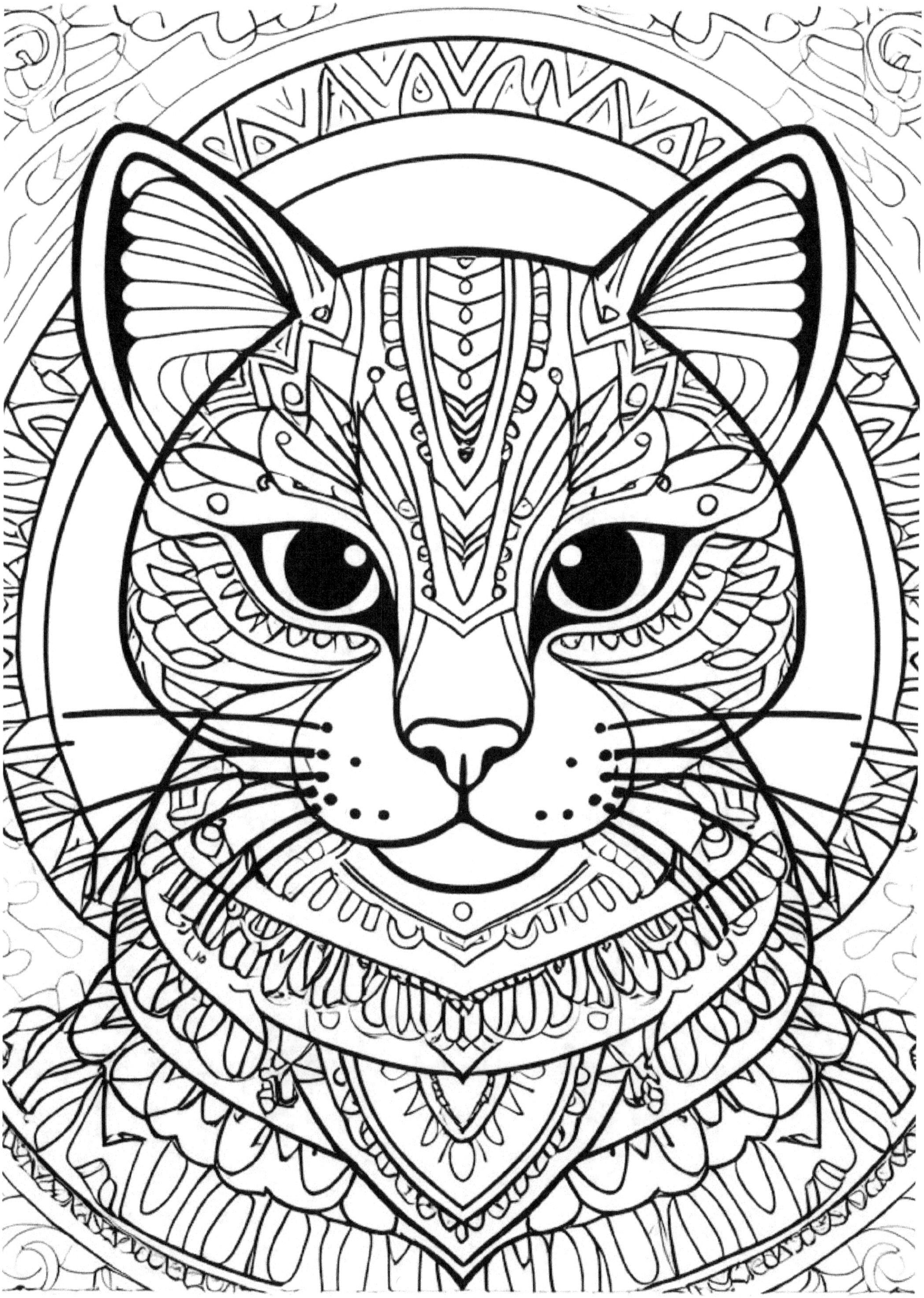

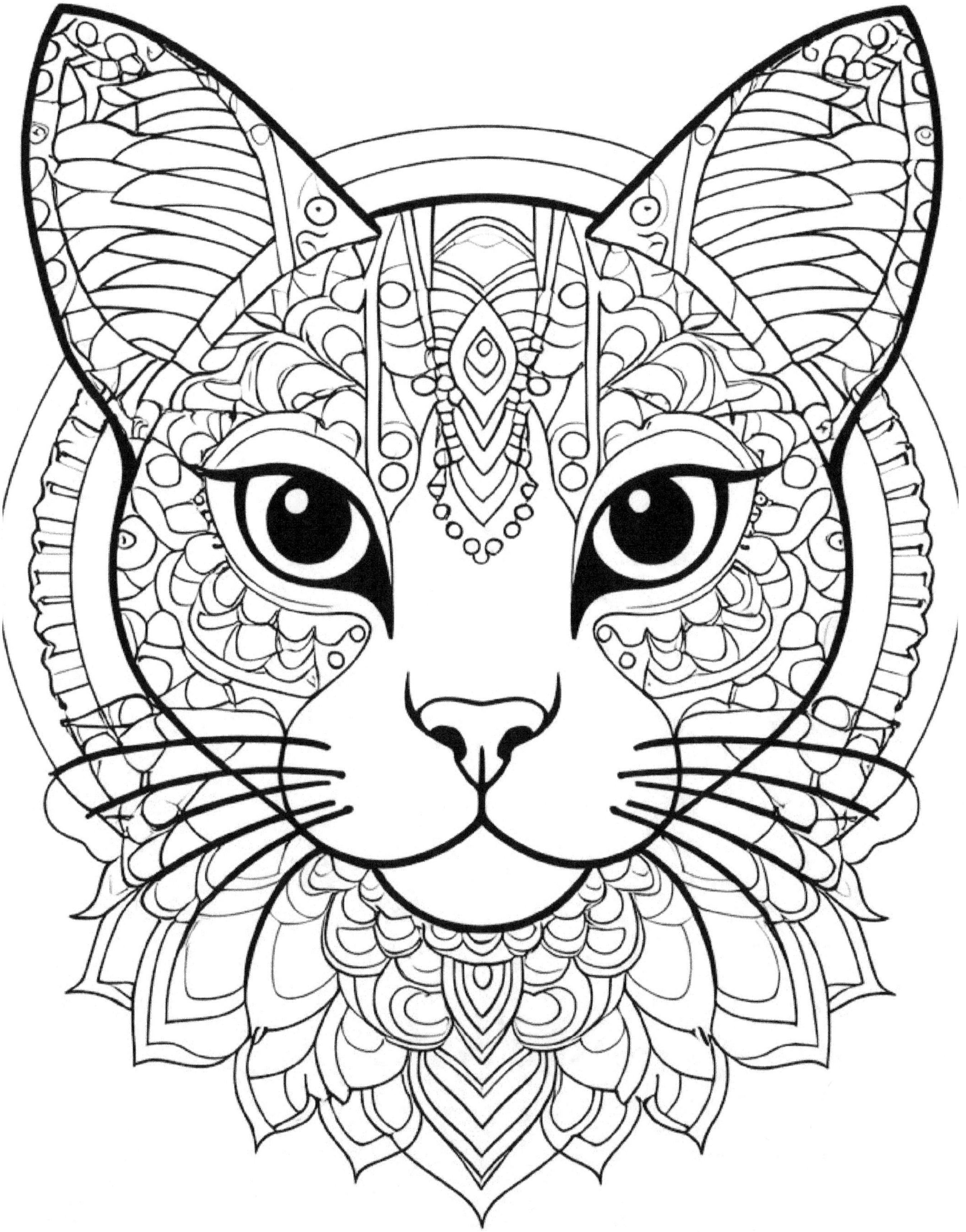

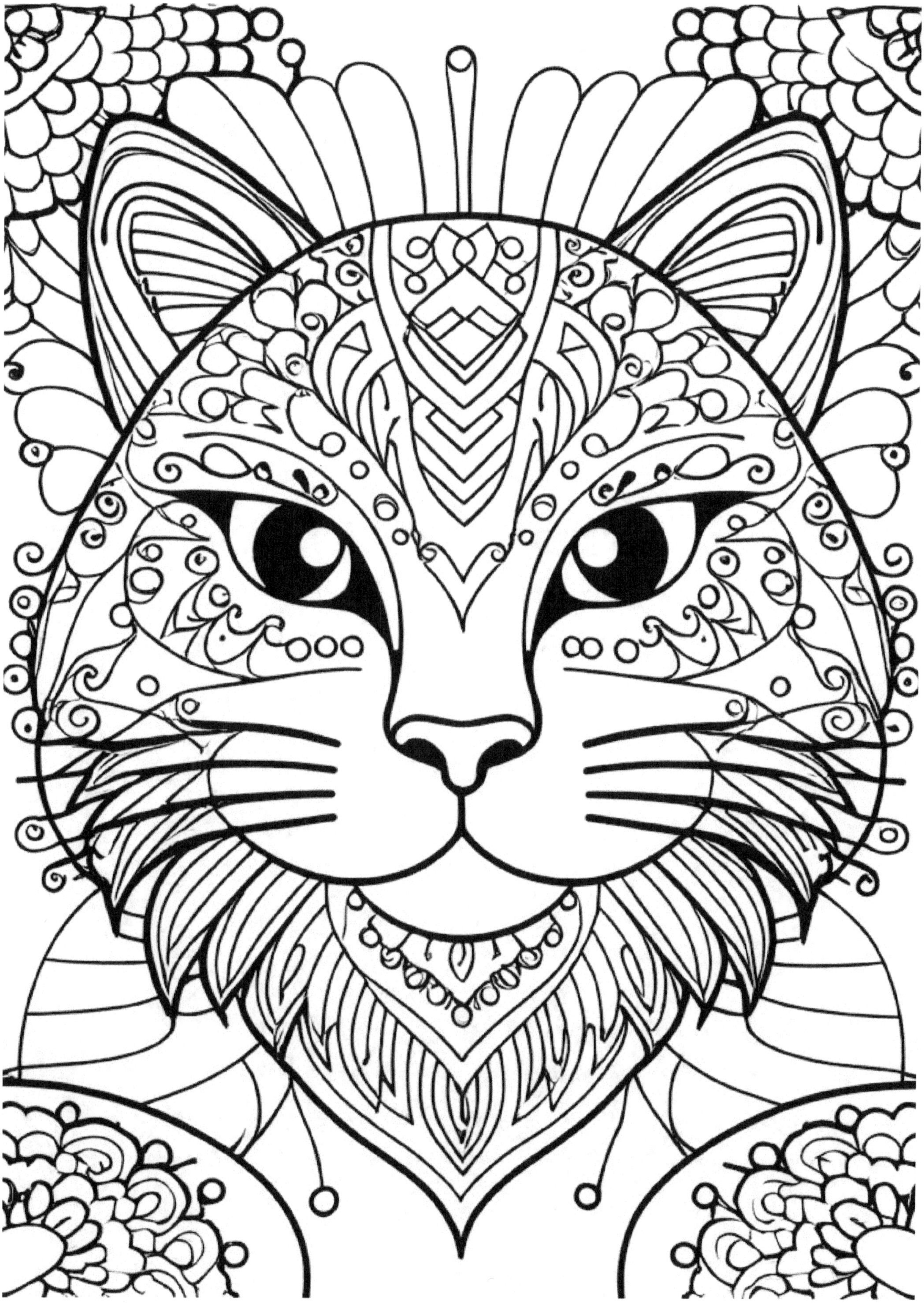

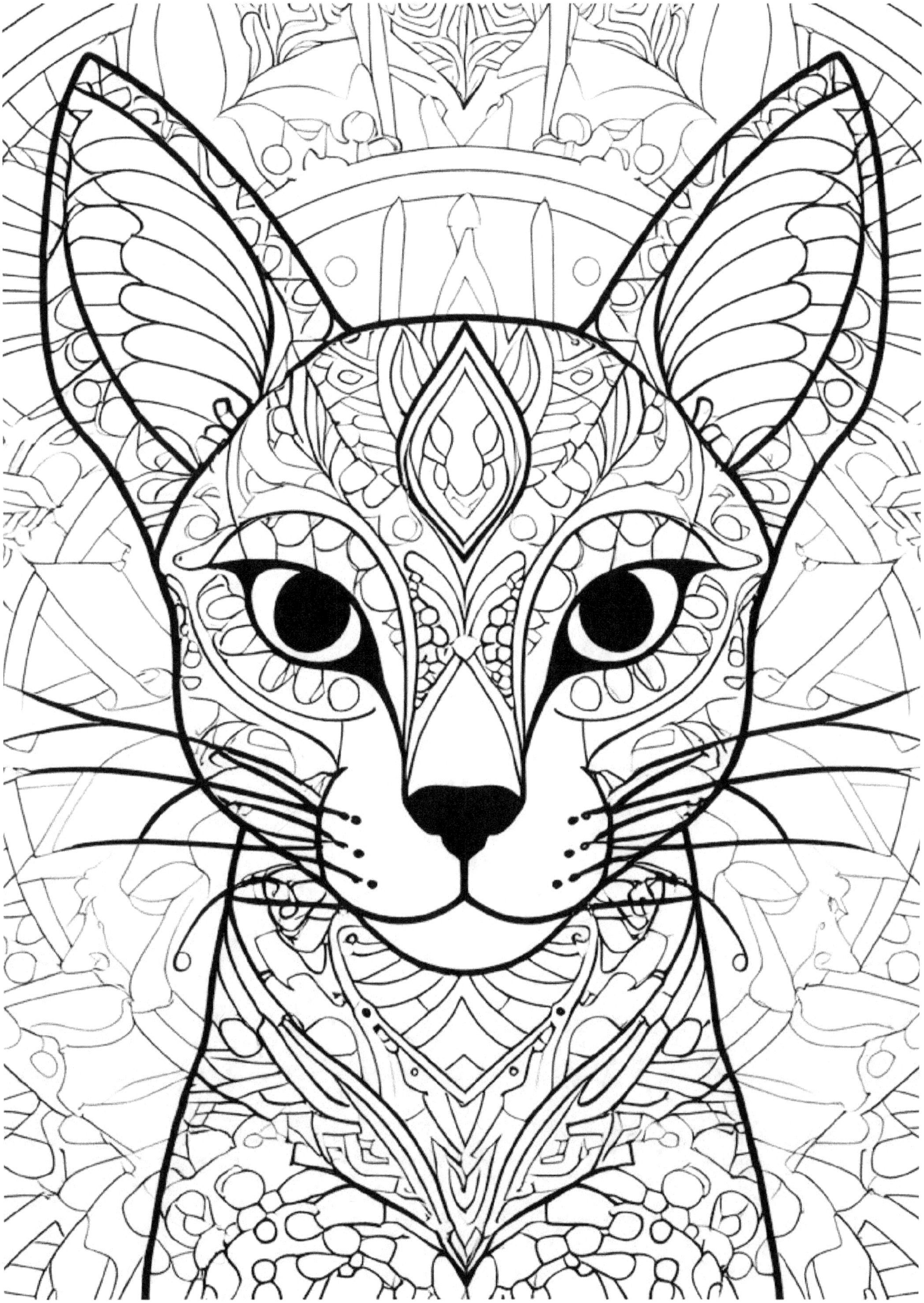

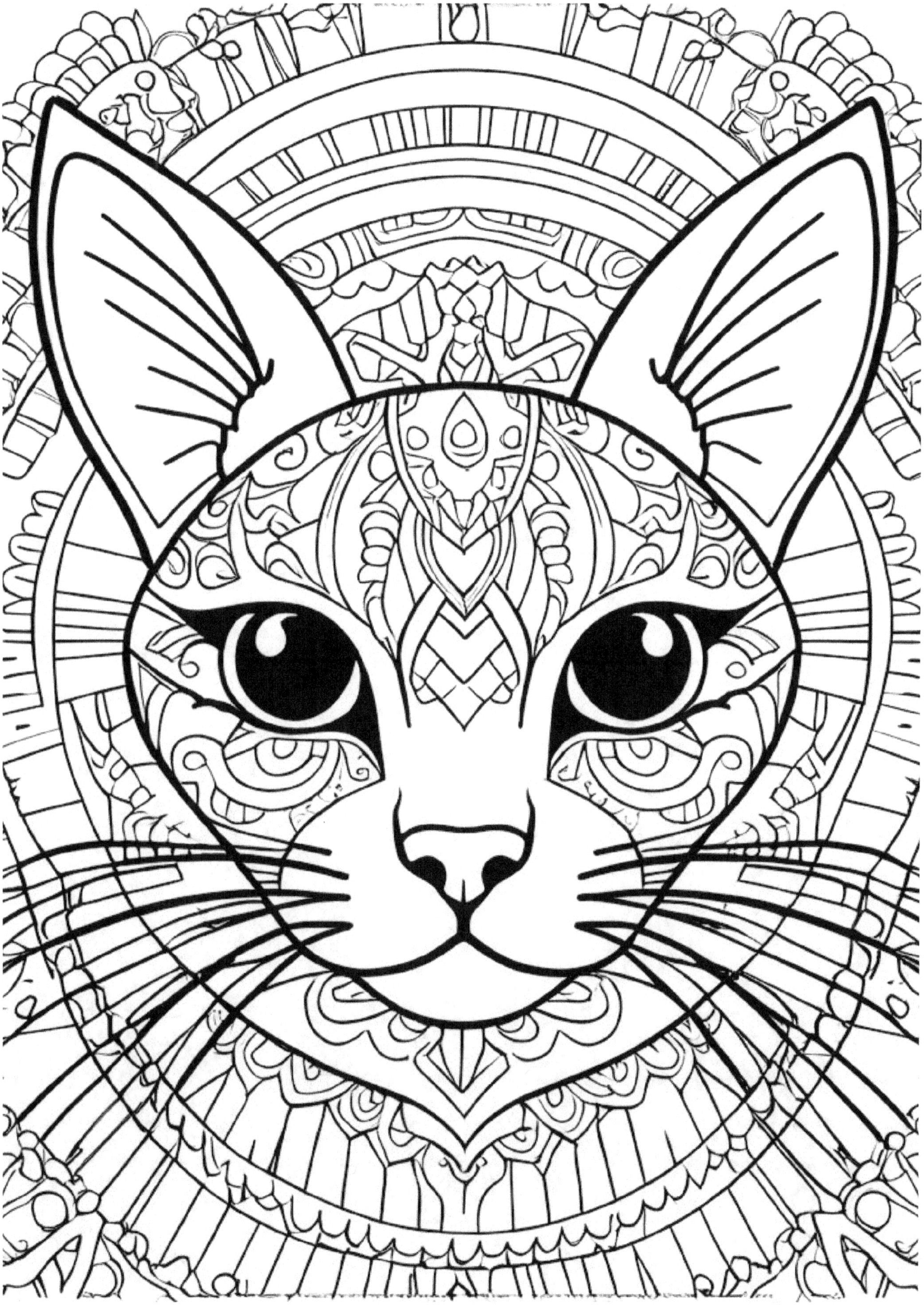

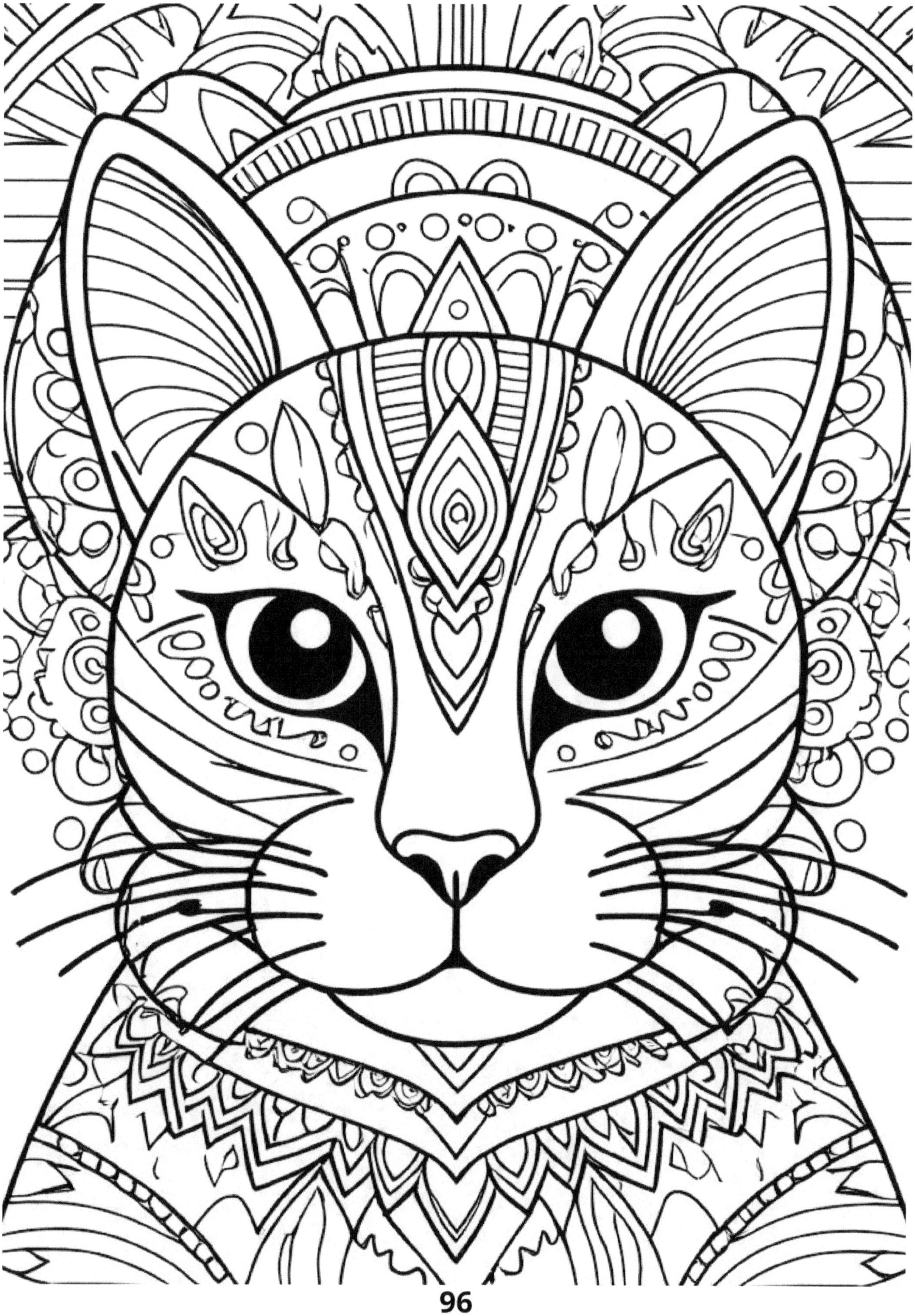

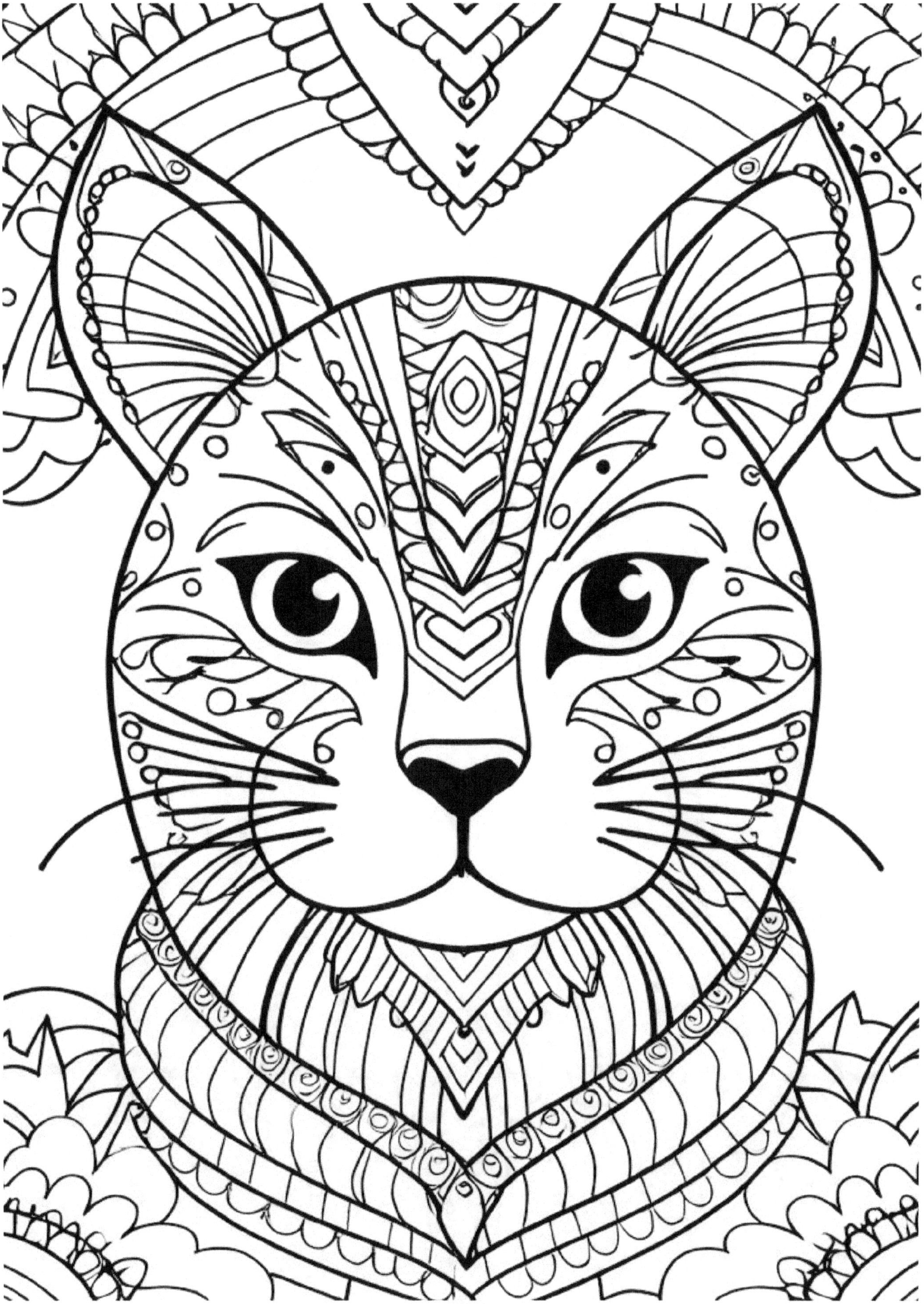

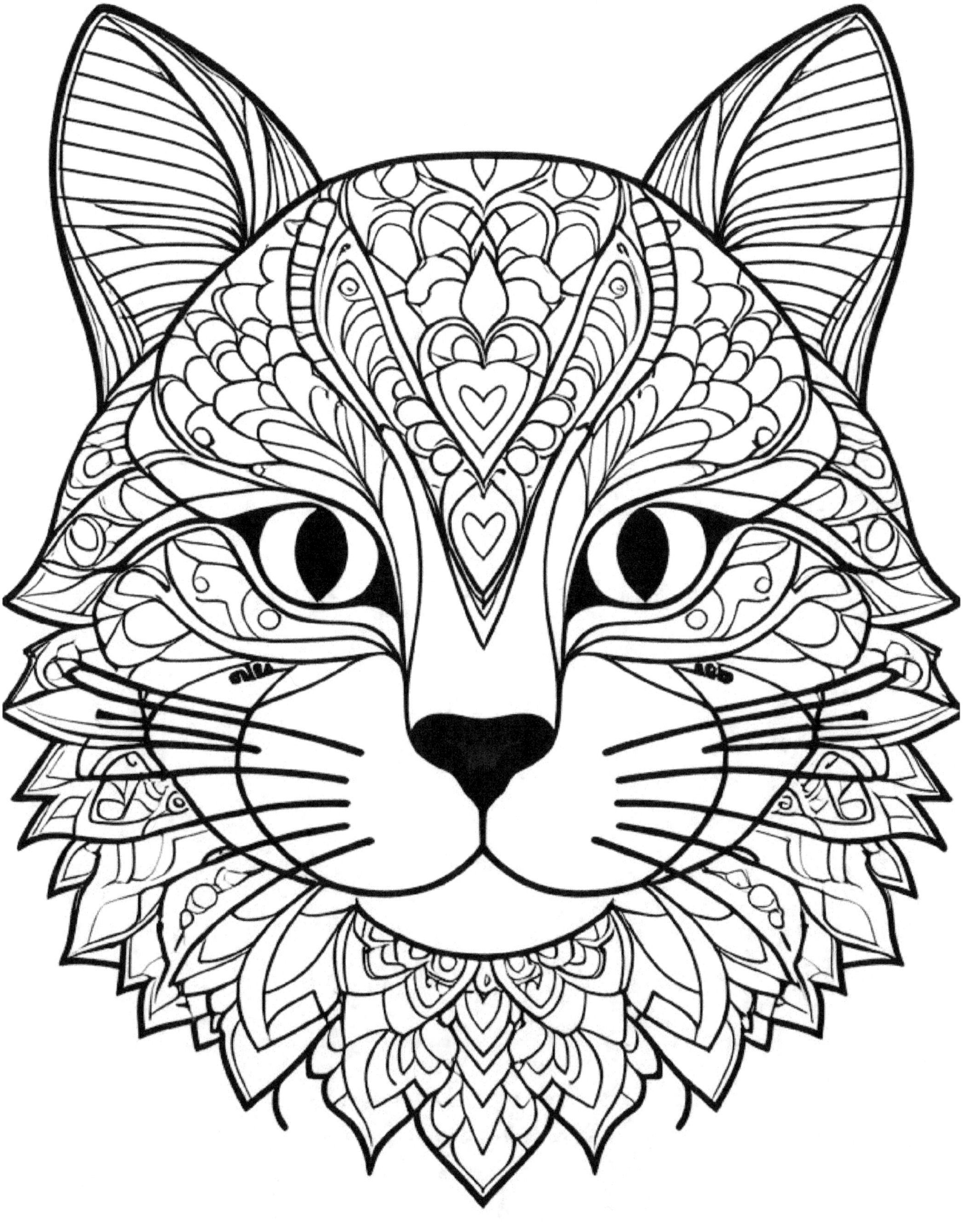

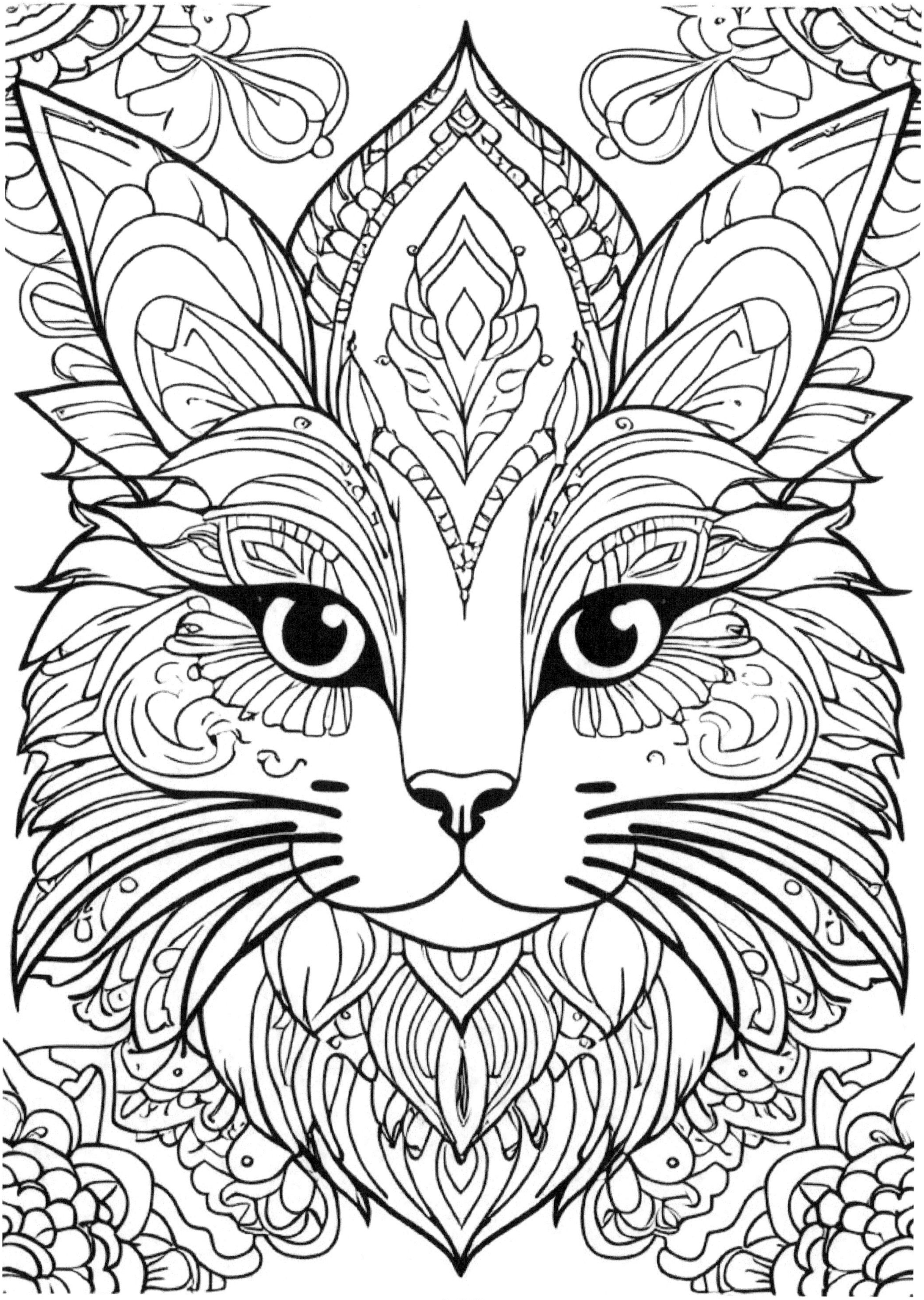

www.ingramcontent.com/pod-product-compliance
Lightning Source LLC
Chambersburg PA
CBHW062113220526
45471CB00010B/3717